Asperger Syndrome
and Social
Relationships

also in the series

Aspies on Mental Health
Speaking for Ourselves
Edited by Luke Beardon and Dean Worton
ISBN 978 1 84905 152 1

Asperger Syndrome and Employment
Adults Speak Out about Asperger Syndrome
Edited by Genevieve Edmonds and Luke Beardon
ISBN 978 1 84310 648 7

of related interest

A Self-Determined Future with Asperger Syndrome
Solution Focused Approaches
E. Veronica Bliss and Genevieve Edmonds
Foreword by Bill O'Connell, Director of Training, Focus on Solutions
ISBN 978 1 84310 513 8

Social Skills for Teenagers and Adults with Asperger Syndrome
A Practical Guide to Day-to-Day Life
Nancy J. Patrick
ISBN 978 1 84310 876 4

The Complete Guide to Asperger's Syndrome
Tony Attwood
Hardback ISBN 978 1 84310 495 7
Paperback ISBN 978 1 84310 669 2

Coming Out Asperger
Diagnosis, Disclosure and Self-Confidence
Edited by Dinah Murray
ISBN 978 1 84310 240 3

Survival Strategies for People on the Autism Spectrum
Marc Fleisher
ISBN 978 1 84310 261 8

Asperger Syndrome
and Social
Relationships

Adults Speak Out about Asperger Syndrome

Edited by Genevieve Edmonds and Luke Beardon

Jessica Kingsley *Publishers*
London and Philadelphia

First published in 2008
by Jessica Kingsley Publishers
116 Pentonville Road
London N1 9JB, UK
and
400 Market Street, Suite 400
Philadelphia, PA 19106, USA

www.jkp.com

Copyright © Jessica Kingsley Publishers 2008
Printed digitally since 2011

Library of Congress Cataloging in Publication Data
A CIP catalog record for this book is available from the Library of Congress

British Library Cataloguing in Publication Data
A CIP catalogue record for this book is available from the British Library

ISBN 978 1 84310 647 0

Contents

Acknowledgements

To all the authors contributing to the series – many thanks for your time and effort in helping to produce these books.

Dedication

To all those individuals with AS who have shared their lives with us; we are forever indebted to you all. (Genevieve Edmonds and Luke Beardon)

Preface to the Series

Genevieve Edmonds

As an adult with Asperger Syndrome (AS) and as someone who works within the field of autism as a trainer and consultant, I am all too aware of the situation facing adults with AS at present. For many (the majority, in reality), it is not good: it is characterized by a lack of understanding, support, respect and appropriate services. The aim of this book series is to make available the experiences of adults with AS on pertinent life issues, so that services and individuals may be able to learn what to do to set up and improve support systems for them.

More people are being diagnosed with Autism Spectrum Disorder (ASD) now than ever before, though the question remains unanswered whether this is as a result of an 'autism epidemic' or as a result of better diagnostic expertise. We do know that autism is a lifelong condition (it doesn't end at the age of 18) with no known cure. Although some tried and tested models of support do exist, there are few which address the needs of adults with AS. Much of the research available around autism appears to be centred around the origins of autism rather than looking at the reality of living with it.

Existing services appear to be guided predominantly by the well-known 'Triad of Impairments' model of autism (Wing and Gould 1979), which outlines the three areas of difficulty (though we should be looking at difference). It leaves adults with AS at the centre of a model that generates deficit-based, rather than person-centred, thinking and approaches. This purely medicalized view of AS is in fact at odds with the intentions of the Government in the UK. In 2006, a note was written to clarify the current picture for individuals with ASDs in transition and adulthood, 'Better Services for people with Autistic Spectrum Disorders (ASD)' (Department of Health 2006). It encourages social care organizations to develop local agendas for service improvement for adults with ASD.

What is needed is a move away from a medicalized view of autism and AS; individuals with AS should be understood as people who process the social world 'differently' rather than in a 'disordered' fashion, and support should centre around the understanding that the *disability* element of AS is born from individuals' lack of *opportunity* to process information differently, and in a way that makes sense to them. Our hope is that with the help of this series better support can begin to emerge for adults with AS so that they can begin to live more fulfilled and happier lives, which sadly too few do at this time.

Bibliography

Department of Health (2006) 'Better services for people with Autistic Spectrum Disorders (ASD)'. Available at www.dh.gov.uk/en/Publicationsandstatistics/ Publications/PublicationsPolicyAndGuidance/DH_065242. Accessed 2 October 2007.

Wing, L. and Gould, J. (1979) 'Severe impairments of social interaction aud associated abnormalities in children: Epidemiology and classification.' *Journal of Autism and Childhood Schizophrenia*, 9, 11–29.

Introduction

Luke Beardon

The following quotation is a refreshing and enlightening perspective that all NTs (neurotypicals) should take into account:

> Neurotypical syndrome is a neurobiological disorder characterized by preoccupation with social concerns, delusions of superiority, and obsession with conformity. Neurotypical individuals often assume that their experience of the world is either the only one, or the only correct one. NTs find it difficult to be alone. NTs are often intolerant of seemingly minor differences in others. When in groups NTs are socially and behaviourally rigid, and frequently insist upon the performance of dysfunctional, destructive, and even impossible rituals as a way of maintaining group identity. NTs find it difficult to communicate directly, and have a much higher incidence of lying as compared to persons on the autistic spectrum. (Institute for the Study of the Neurologically Typical, http://isnt.autistics.org, accessed 11 February 2008.)

The writings of people with autism or Asperger Syndrome (AS) can never be replaced for their value in bringing into the world a greater insight into what it is like to have an autism condition. What can be found in this volume is a wide-ranging set of views from individuals with AS commenting on and sharing their experiences of the social world. In many chapters you will find hints or suggestions for people with AS to assist in developing and maintaining social relationships. As a person who does not have AS, I would not undermine theses in any way; however, there is very little in this book that refers directly to NTs – what their responsibility is in developing social relationships with people with AS. If it is to be accepted (embraced, welcomed would be preferable) that people with AS are certainly equal to NTs, if not surpassing them in many qualities – and, surely this is an ethos that should be adopted sooner rather than later – then it seems to me that the next logical step would be to recognize that responsibilities lie just as much with the NT population as with those with AS to adjust NT behaviour in order to make social situations less stressful and more bearable to people with AS. There are many texts written about how to develop and 'change' people with AS to make individuals more socially acceptable. Now, hang on – what does socially acceptable mean? Whatever it does mean, one could reasonably expect that the definition has been based purely on NT perspective, ethos, morality and judgement. And who are NTs to assume that this judgement is correct? I know many individuals with AS (in fact I would include almost everyone I know with AS in this) who would suggest that many behaviours of NTs can cause major distress and offence to them. Why is it that the majority of NTs are obsessed with changing people with AS to be more like them, rather than thinking harder about how they might change to be more AS friendly? I am not one who would suggest that people with AS do not require support in developing skills in order that they are more accepted and able to follow pathways that are meaningful to them – as, indeed, are people without AS – but I do find it frustrating that it seems almost invariable that it is the person with AS who has to make the sacrifices, while their NT counterparts are not expected to change in any way. I use the term 'sacrifice' in a very real sense; often I get the impression (sometimes more than an impression when I get to know someone well) that people with AS are essentially being asked (or told) that they have to give up their very own sense of self and way of being, simply in order to 'get on' in the NT world. How many NTs would sit back and accept that? How many NTs would make the effort to change their very selves in such a fundamental manner? No wonder so many individuals with AS become reclusive, withdrawn – simply to avoid the NT world that is so potentially (and actually) damaging to their selves and their way of being. And yet these same individuals are often told that they *must* engage in the outside world, that it is a *good* thing, that social interaction is a *positive* thing. According to many people I speak to it's not. This is not to say that engaging in the outside (NT) world can not be good and positive – certainly it can. But I tend to find that when it is good and positive the reasons behind it stem (inevitably?) from NTs making adjustments and changing their expectations to better suit the individual with AS. So, this concept is less about how people with AS 'need' to change, and more about how NTs should shoulder at least some of the responsibility. On this point, many people argue to me that it is incredibly difficult to change and adapt to better suit people with AS – I, for one, would not argue against that. I would, however, point out that however difficult it is for NTs, I suspect it is immeasurably harder for those with AS.

I suspect that one of the (main) reasons that many NTs find the behaviours of people with AS so bewildering is that the issues that the individual with AS is consciously aware of are often only ever present in the subconscious part of the NT brain. Therefore, NTs simply do not consciously think about the very issues that people with AS can have major problems with. Take a (stereo) typical example of a woman asking her partner, on trying on a new pair of jeans – 'Does my bum look big in this?' Now, any NT male with half a brain would not even take the time to look at his partner's derrière – it is an immediate stock response along the lines of 'Of course not, you've got a lovely arse' – or similar. Naturally, this, taken logically, is highly ridiculous. First, why would a woman ask such a question – after all, mirrors were invented for a specific purpose and she has a perfectly good set of eyes – if she really wants to know, go and look in the mirror and stop bothering me when I've got better things to do? Second, if the *honest* answer to the question is actually a resounding 'YES – stop eating so much cheese and it might help!' then why would such a response be greeted with frostiness (at best) or a major relationship breakdown at worst? Do NTs not actually want honesty? If not, why ask the question in the first place? This simply highlights the extraordinary lack of honest logic that NTs are capable of – from an AS perspective this could be extremely difficult to understand. Of course, the whole scenario is actually more complex that it seems – perhaps the female in question is subtly (or not so subtly) asking for affirmation of her partner's feelings towards her. Maybe she is giving him a chance to make up for an earlier faux pas. Whatever the reason, it is easy from an NT perspective to see the wider picture. But does it revolve around logic and honesty from the perspective of someone with AS? Almost surely not. So, with that in mind, adopting a more honest and logical approach to relationships (in whatever format) with people with AS is likely to benefit the relationship enormously. Unfortunately, many NT individuals find it so difficult to be direct and, indeed, honest – but, believe me, it can do wonders for people with AS and is actually not that difficult with a bit of practice (or even, God forbid, a behavioural programme...).

I am asked so many times by people with AS – what, exactly, is a friend? It is nigh on an impossible question to answer, as it may mean something different depending on who is asking the question. There is no simple, concrete answer to what is, essentially, a fairly abstract question. After all, many NTs would use the same term to describe a range of different people – all of whom they actually have a different relationship with. So, what can NTs do to try and reduce the problems that an NT/AS friendship may pose? First, I would suggest that honesty is a critical policy. If someone with AS genuinely asks an NT individual, 'Can I be your friend?', so often, the answer (to spare any feelings, or as a result of not knowing what else to say) will be 'OK then, yes'. However, this can give rise to major problems – in some extreme cases leading to cautions from the police (not to the NT, who could be seen as 'leading the person with AS on', but to the person with AS him/herself for simply behaving in a way that is natural to them). In such circumstances it should be established just what the individual means by 'friend' – often, the NT may be surprised at the definition, but at least then the options are a lot clearer. Many individuals with AS are 'all or nothing' – a trait which is immensely positive in many ways. Boundaries need to be established so that neither party ends up disillusioned or upset – and this should be just as much the responsibility of the NT as the individual with AS.

One of the many things that NTs find hard to accept is the concept that being alone – or being in company but not 'joining in' – can be fantastic. NTs seem to have an inbuilt system that craves company, and suggests that when in company talking is a must. This is blatantly not true for some individuals with AS who may be perfectly comfortable with enjoying company without talking; or, at least, comfort would be achieved if the NT social pressure of having to talk was alleviated. Almost invariably if the NT 'rules' are followed then the communication (from the NT perspective) tends to be wholly social – the antithesis in many cases of what might make a person with AS feel at ease. Alternatively, if the conversation is led by the individual with AS they may choose (totally logically) to chat about what interests them. Should this topic of conversation not be appealing to those around them once again they find themselves having 'done the wrong thing' – how is an individual to 'win' in such a situation!? I think that moving away from this idea that to enjoy company one *has* to talk could only benefit people with AS. Clearly this is not something that is going to happen overnight – nor should it, it is part of what makes up the complex NT tapestry of being; however, it should also be very much taken into account in an NT/AS relationship if it is to be successful.

'Directness' can be seen in both a positive and negative light. NTs teach their children to 'tell the truth' – and then admonish then for stating Granny's chin is hairy. NTs sometimes admire the propensity of the levels of honesty found in people with AS – while at the same time trying to teach them not to be so blunt. Surely it is not so difficult to see why such a contradictory attitude causes so many problems for people with AS? I know of very few people with AS who deliberately set out to cause offence or to upset someone else – quite the opposite, in fact. And yet many of these same individuals are being taught that they should not say what they think…except in certain situations; and it's a good thing to tell the truth…mostly, anyway; and do what you are told…well, actually it depends on what you are being told to do and who is telling you; be yourself…as long as it fits in with what we want…and so on – and on. For individuals who are quite rule bound and find it problematic *intuitively* to know what to do, when and why, it is hardly surprising that the NT world can be utterly confusing to the point of driving them off the edge. If only the NT world was consistent, that would be a great start. Obviously this is not going to happen, as most of the world (at present, at least) is populated by NTs – but, in a social relationship of two people, it is not too much to suggest that there be some consistency in 'telling the truth' – and being direct and honest.

This leads me onto perhaps what I regard as the most important aspect of any relationship with someone with AS – be it a parent/child relationship, a friendship or a partner relationship – and that is the one of trust. Trust, it could be said, is the basis of any good relationship. However, many NT relationships are based on mutual trust which is not often overtly expressed. In many cases, it does not become an issue unless a trust has been broken in some way. For people with AS trust can often either be something won very easily, or which takes a lot of time and effort to gain. The former example is often found in individuals who have yet to learn that people are not always trustworthy – that sometimes (often) people do not say exactly what they mean, and that someone's word often is not their bond. Such individuals need to be treated very carefully in order for their trust in an individual not to be disappointed. The latter example tends to be found in individuals who have almost given up on NT 'dishonesty' – it can be very difficult to know who to trust when so many times in the past the individual has been let down, lied to or treated in an unexpected way. If an individual is going to be honest and direct with you, I feel that the same courtesy should be shown to them. A lot of this is about thinking very carefully about what you are going to say prior to actually saying it, to ensure that there can be no ambiguity or misinterpretation. Additionally, I think that taking the perspective of the individual with AS (as far as is possible) can dramatically change the way in which a relationship can develop. For example, rather than thinking that someone is merely irritating because they seem to talk about their own interests all of the time, take a look at their perspective – high levels of social anxiety, low levels of intuitive understanding of the complex rules of social engagement, a logical desire to avoid meaningless topics – and, sometimes, this can be enough for you to realize that the individual is not being deliberately self-orientating, but is genuinely engaging with you. Once gained, trust from a person with AS should be guarded closely; once lost, it can be extremely difficult to regain. I also believe that the longer the relationship of trust, the more able the individual with AS is able to cope when mistakes are made. The world is not an ideal place and such things will happen – the stronger the trusting bond, the stronger the relationship, the more likely it is that the relationship will survive.

It is not possible, in a few brief words, to cover everything that can be said about social relationships. Not everything I have written will be applicable to every neurotypical person – nor every person with AS – indeed there will be individuals out there for whom little, or none of this is relevant. It would not be possible, with any document, however lengthy, to cover all people. What I hoped to gain from writing this is to suggest that NTs have a huge impact on people with AS, and the better NTs are at adapting their own social behaviour when it comes to relationships, the better it will be for people with AS. And, I personally believe, that the more NT/AS friendships and relationships there are that flourish, the better it is for all concerned.

Editors' note

There are many different ways of describing people with AS/autism. Use of terminology is very individual – while some individuals may describe themselves as a person with autism/AS, others may say they are autistic people or an aspie, or use some other variant. As these chapters have been written by individuals on the spectrum themselves we have left original terminology unchanged, but would like it noted that each individual has the right to describe him/herself in ways that suit them; we do not wish to cause any offence to any individual within the population.

Chapter 1: One-Channel Communication: Developing Social Relations Online

Chris Mitchell

Introduction by Luke Beardon

Chris writes eloquently about the pros and cons of online communication for individuals with AS. So many individuals have had bad experiences in the NT world, particularly in social situations. Many professionals do not realize that sociability has nothing whatsoever to do with intuitive social understanding – I suspect that the same range of sociability (i.e. need for and wanting social relationships – friends, relationships) is similar to that of the NT population. Some individuals will be happy with just one good friend, others strive to have many. However, as a result of the problems faced in the NT world it is good to see the internet being used in such a way as to be beneficial to those with AS. Not only, as Chris points out, does online communication reduce or eliminate many of the related difficulties such as non-verbal communication, it can also be used as a wide resource to make contact with like-minded people.

Key issues clearly are those of safety – online can be a dangerous place, particularly if the next step is taken to meet up in person. However, I think that overall online communication offers more than compensatory attributes. From a personal perspective as an NT I have found that my friendships with people with AS flourish via email contact, while in person we can relax in the happy knowledge that we don't have to say anything at all, unless we really want to!

The internet is for many high-function autistics what sign language is for the deaf (Dekker 1998). Almost by coincidence, the number of individuals being diagnosed with Asperger Syndrome has risen alongside widening access to internet communication. Internet access has enabled Asperger communities around the world to discover themselves in a way that previously would not have been possible. As the Asperger population is so small compared to the total world population and is thinly spread rather than clustered together (Baron-Cohen, Saunders and Chakrabarti 1999), opportunities for many people with Asperger Syndrome to meet up are often limited. The internet has the ability to unite such thinly spread communities. This chapter looks at the benefits internet access and communication can have for people diagnosed with Asperger Syndrome as well as problems it may also have, including isolation.

Not only has internet access enabled the Asperger community to discover itself in such a way, it has also provided an effective communication tool for many individuals diagnosed with the condition, especially since many often experience difficulties with face-to-face and verbal communication media. As these communication media are multi-channel, an individual with Asperger Syndrome may experience 'sensory overload'. Sensory overload in many individuals with Asperger Syndrome can result from:

- the presence of too many people and voices in a social situation

- having to tune into so many channels associated with verbal/face-to-face communication including:
  - eye contact
  - tone of voice
  - facial expression.

The one-channel mono-text nature of internet communication via email removes these barriers, making communication more manageable for many with Asperger Syndrome, thus opening up opportunities to develop social interaction skills. Another advantage that email communication has for many people with Asperger Syndrome is that they can go along at their own pace in terms of thinking about structuring a reply to an email.

In verbal and face-to-face situations, many people with Asperger Syndrome find that as well as having to balance other social cues with communication, it can also be difficult to think quickly enough of what to say as an appropriate response, which can lead to them saying something unintentionally offensive. Though NTs can also produce comments that are either unhelpful or offensive to a person with Asperger Syndrome, for the person with Asperger Syndrome, it can be difficult to understand when and if they have made such an inappropriate comment. Sadly, this can cause social misunderstandings in that others may jump to erroneous conclusions about the person with Asperger Syndrome, even when the person with Asperger Syndrome is trying his or her best to get along with others.

Depending upon the individual with Asperger Syndrome, possibilities that interaction through email offers include the following:

- People with Asperger Syndrome who often experience such social isolation may develop a desire to go beyond the limitations of email communication and meet email respondents in person.

- Alternatively, some individuals with Asperger Syndrome have obsessive-compulsive tendencies and may become over-reliant on internet use to the point where it could possibly isolate them from most forms of personal contact.

As the first possibility suggests, regular use of email communication can be a step towards developing social skills that can eventually translate to verbal and face-to-face situations. By subscribing to emailing lists for people with Asperger Syndrome and related conditions, many appear to feel less isolated and that they have learned more about themselves from others who often share similar issues and concerns. In turn, it enables them to apply new skills to cope with recurring problems in their daily life. Subscribers to autism emailing lists, online forums etc., often use such facilities to share advice and tips on how to handle face-to-face and verbal social situations. Elsewhere, some people with Asperger Syndrome have, via online facilities, also found out about social groups and other services near where they live where they can meet others in person and develop effective interpersonal skills.

Many individuals with Asperger Syndrome, who perhaps previously lacked confidence in developing social relations, appear to have found a way to participate in social situations where face-to-face, verbal and body language is present. The author of this chapter, through subscription to an emailing list for university students, was encouraged to travel to Australia to meet friends developed through online communication. Martijn Dekker, founder of the Independent Living on the Autistic Spectrum (INLV) list, one of the first emailing lists for people with Asperger Syndrome, took a two-month visit to the United States to meet other subscribers he met through the list he had started. An interesting observation Dekker made on communication between people with Asperger Syndrome, is that many use little verbal or body language, mainly using words and saying what they have to say in its entirety without filling in silences with small-talk. In this sense, face-to-face conversations between people with Asperger Syndrome can almost resemble written communication (Dekker 1998).

However, not all aspects of this opportunity are positive. A person with Asperger Syndrome, especially if they are very literal in terms of interpretation, may not initially realize that people online may not be who they say they are. This could present a problem if a person with Asperger Syndrome decides to meet a respondent who may have provided false information about him/herself shortly after meeting them through email. Due to the limits email communication presents, it is very difficult to find out about a respondent's personality. Without any form of social cues present, it is very difficult for anyone to tell if a respondent is lying – and this is a problem with email communication which everyone faces, not just those with Asperger Syndrome. As many people with Asperger Syndrome can be rather literal in their ways of thought, they may believe much, if not everything, they see or read online. You should always be careful not to give out too much personal information.

The availability of online Asperger Syndrome diagnosis can also have an indirect effect on social interaction online among the Asperger community. If an online diagnosis is obtained from a genuine, well-policed site there shouldn't be much problem, but there is still much misinformation about Asperger Syndrome online. It is possible that people with an online Asperger Syndrome diagnosis may turn out not to have Asperger Syndrome at all, but instead have a personality disorder. A person with a genuine diagnosis can be vulnerable to this.

As some individuals with Asperger Syndrome may have obsessive-compulsive tendencies, excessive dependence on internet/email communication can lead to isolation and eventually the almost total abandonment of life outside the computer. This issue can also apply to people who don't have Asperger Syndrome. It is well documented that people have lost their families and their jobs through such isolation.

Though internet communication presents so many advantages to many people with Asperger Syndrome as it can mask the demands that verbal and face-to-face communication can present, it is also a restrictive medium and cannot talk for ever. Some may feel comfortable online, but others may find that they want to go beyond the online to develop more personal, and in some cases, even intimate relationships. Each preference must be respected.

There follow some suggestions for enabling successful transition of development of social skills from online environments to social situations and to avoid excessive dependency on internet/email communication.

Choosing and joining an online environment for people with Asperger Syndrome

Online environments for people with Asperger Syndrome are available in the forms of emailing lists, chat rooms, online forums, bulletin/message boards etc. The choice of such facilities is very wide and varied, and as a result can appear confusing:

- Locating an Asperger online community can be confusing, though there are some 'gateways' to online autism resources that can direct internet users to an online Asperger community including:
  - Online Autism Information Service (OASIS)
  - The ASC Good Practice Guide.

- Not all online Asperger communities are specifically for people on the autistic spectrum, as some may be more parent/professional orientated. Discussion topics on such lists may be difficult for people on the autistic spectrum to relate to.

- Before subscribing to an online Asperger community, it may be helpful to contact the organizer to find out about the general purpose of the community and the themes of discussion that take place within the community.

As mentioned, there is much misinformation about autism and Asperger Syndrome. It is therefore important that one develops and applies the necessary skills to be able to think critically to be able to make effective judgements of online material. When choosing online Asperger communities:

- It may be useful to note if an online Asperger community you are interested in is recognized by a legitimate autism organization (e.g. the National Autistic Society, Asperger Syndrome Foundation etc.) or is listed in a reliable autism information portal (e.g. OASIS, PARIS); this suggests its connection/interest in autism is more likely to be genuine.

- It may also help to make a note of the address of the community when judging between what is genuine and misinformation. For instance, if an address finishes with .co.uk, .org.uk, the organizer has to apply stating the purpose of their site.

- When subscribing to an online Asperger community, make sure that the community has a set of ground rules to ensure where possible a safe and confidential environment.

Communicating within an online Asperger community

Though many participants in online Asperger communities feel comfortable in such environments, being able to talk to others who share similar issues and concerns, friction can still take place with online Asperger communities. Such friction often occurs in the form of 'flaming' (where a subscriber deliberately posts offensive or even malicious comments). For subscribers with Asperger Syndrome, it can often be very difficult to recognize when they are unintentionally offending or even flaming:

- Due to often literal interpretations, degrees of which vary between individuals with Asperger Syndrome, it is possible that one subscriber may interpret another's posting as an insult or, in some cases, even a threat.

- Alternatively, it may be difficult for a subscriber to understand how other subscribers may interpret their messages.

Many online Asperger communities have ground rules to ensure that such actions are kept to a minimum, and some even de-subscribe subscribers if they are found to be posting such comments or are seen as being a threat to the safe and confidential nature of the community. To avoid falling into such traps, it may help if you are a subscriber to do the following:

- Where possible, try to avoid cynicism or sarcasm, as such comments can easily be interpreted by subscribers with Asperger Syndrome as patronizing or offensive.

- If you feel, for any reason, what you may have to say may cause friction or offence, it may be best not to post it to your respective community. If you are unsure though, it may be best to email the community owner/administrator first.

- If you unintentionally post a comment that turns out to be offensive to some subscribers (which can be done very easily), it may help to ask for mediation from the community/administrator, so that whoever you have unintentionally insulted has confirmation that it wasn't intentional.

As a subscriber to an online Asperger community, you could also find yourself on the receiving end of such postings.

- If you feel a subscriber has offended you, intentionally or unintentionally, don't react angrily or personally as this may cause further friction, which can spread ill-will across the community.

- When you feel that you are being offended or even threatened, contact your community owner/administrator immediately via private email.

Whereas issues such as flaming can have a direct negative effect within an online Asperger community, something that can have a more indirect effect is a topic of conversation being of relevance only to a minority within the community (e.g. between just two or three subscribers). If such minority topics of conversation begin to dominate the community this can present a problem, as other subscribers, to whom such issues don't apply or who can't understand them, can feel excluded. To avoid issues becoming too personal between a select minority of subscribers and to maintain inclusion of all community members where possible, the following may help:

- If a topic of conversation within a community is either personal or of interest to just a few subscribers, it may be best to continue it via private email.

- To maintain inclusion of all community members, when starting a topic of conversation it may help to, at first, ask all list members if a particular issue applies to them, so that they are at least invited to participate.

Beyond the online environment: How to successfully take online social relations into verbal and face-to-face situations

When starting to develop social relations online, it is important to remember that respondents may not always be who they say they are online. Steps to take to successfully translate an online social relationship into a personal relationship include the following:

- Do not rush into meeting a respondent in person, and consider your safety carefully if and when you eventually decide to meet.

- Before planning to meet a respondent in person, it is important to communicate with them via other media where possible:
  - so that you can develop perhaps more reciprocal conversations, it may help to communicate via MSN or ICQ
  - to develop verbal reciprocal conversations, it may help to contact a respondent via telephone where possible
  - verbal and face-to-face interaction can be practised using webcams and microphones.

The most important thing is always to consider your safety. There continue to be cases of individuals using the internet for sinister purposes: some invent lies about who they are in their online correspondence and one cannot tell whether or not they are trustworthy. If you decide to meet a respondent in person, you should meet in a public place, rather than in your own home or theirs. You, should consider asking a friend to accompany you when you first meet a respondent, and always let somebody (a friend or family member, for example) know of your plans, including where you're going and when you intend to get home.

Bibliography

Baron-Cohen, S., Saunders, K. and Chakrabarti, S. (1999) 'Does autism cluster geographically? A research note.' *Autism 5* (1), 39–43.

Dekker, M. (1998) 'On our own terms: Emerging cultures'. Unpuplished paper.

Chapter 2: Developing a Better Social Understanding

Steve Jarvis

Introduction by Luke Beardon

I want to note three areas that Steve highlights in this chapter. First, that it would be helpful to have specific counselling for support post-diagnosis. Having support at this time is crucial – indeed, can be one of the most influencing factors for the way forward for any given individual. My main concern, however, is the distinct lack of professionals who are willing and able to perform such a function. The recognition that levels of global expertise in AS in adult services is poor is long overdue. By global expertise I mean across the range of services, including those in health, social services and the penal system, to note just three. Without this recognition my fear is that adults are going to continue to be unsupported, or supported in a way that is not beneficial to them.

Second, Steve feels that perhaps as a direct result of his academic ability his social and emotional development did not take place, or were not supported. I think that this is a very common theme – yet it takes little thought to realize that social intelligence, emotional intelligence and academic ability are all very separate entities. To be good at one does not automatically mean that you will be good at another. The sooner we understand this the sooner perhaps we can provide education in social and emotional areas, not simply academic education. And, to be fair, I suspect that having good social skills and emotional understanding are far better tools to equip an adult in daily life than is academic understanding.

Last, I wanted to comment on the simple yet excellent way in which Steve uses the television to develop his own skills. What a genius idea!

As a child and as an adult, I lived my life with the assumption that I was normal and I tried to fit in. At school this led me to play the role of 'joker'. I tried to be funny to be part of a group. But this strategy rarely helped me make friends and only served to damage my fragile sense of self-worth. I lacked the self-awareness to understand why I might feel the need to play the 'joker'. Now I think it was because I could not keep up with what was being said, and trying to make others laugh seemed my only way to be accepted by the group. I was fortunate not to receive much bullying as a child, and perhaps this strategy did protect me from being bullied as I provided a valued service to the group. I did not help myself, because all the time I was trying to hide my difficulties from people who might have been able to help me.

My childhood experience has taught me the importance of early diagnosis and support for children with Asperger Syndrome (AS). Parents, teachers and general practitioners (GPs) need to be helped to increase their awareness of AS so they are better able to identify children who might have this condition at an early age. If I had been made aware of my emotional and social difficulties as a child and given coaching and support to address these difficulties, I may have been less tempted to demean myself by playing the role of 'joker'. I think there is a need for far more trained AS counsellors and coaches to provide this service. Developing the skills of emotional intelligence should be given a much greater priority in education, particularly for children diagnosed with autistic spectrum disorder. I am sure I presented the outward appearance of success at school and college because I kept passing exams, but all the time I was slipping behind in terms of the development of the essential emotional and social skills necessary to succeed in social relationships and later in marriage and as a parent.

I had few friends as a child and I was poor at maintaining these friendships into adulthood. At the time I had little idea why this was so. I have been lonely for periods of my adult life as a consequence of not being proactive about socializing to make friends. In part this was a mental health issue, as social anxiety, low self-esteem and depression were barriers to feeling able to act to make new social contacts. I think I also lacked the awareness that I had a need to socialize to help release pent-up emotions and as mitigation against the risk of falling into a depressed state of mind. I found counselling helped me gain this understanding.

As a young adult, I could be easily led in social groups. I got in with the wrong group of people at college and one evening they bought me many alcoholic drinks. They could not understand why I never seemed to change my emotional state when I was drinking – I never seemed to behave drunk. I eventually lost consciousness and I was taken to hospital in an ambulance in a coma with alcohol poisoning. The doctor seemed convinced that I was trying to commit suicide, which certainly was not the case. It must have been a worrying night for my parents. I mention this unfortunate personal experience as a specific example of the dangerous situations that can arise for a person with AS from a lack of self-awareness and social understanding.

I hope you will indulge me at this point as I try to explain the relevance of a well-established model for how people learn. The model describes how we start off as *unconsciously incompetent* at something. If we become aware of this, then we can move to the next stage, which is being *consciously incompetent*. A suitable education or training programme can help us move to the stage of being *consciously competent* and further practice and reinforcement can get us to the final state of *unconsciously competent*. I will use an example of how this model could apply to someone with AS who is struggling to develop social relationships. This could be me as a young adult. I know I bored people by talking at length on subjects that they were not interested in, and this would hinder my attempts to develop friendships. I did eventually acquire some awareness of this and modified my behaviour so I never talked for longer than a few minutes on any topic. I would have benefited from more feedback on the effect I was having. I think this is a common problem for people with AS. We just do not have the awareness of the effect we are having when we talk at length on a subject of interest to us, and we find it difficult to read the body language of the other person to tell whether they are still interested in what we are saying. I do not think it is easy for some people on the autistic spectrum to acquire necessary awareness in this area, but I do know that not enough constructive feedback is given to help raise this awareness. I certainly think that about my experiences as a child and adult with undiagnosed AS. Unfortunately, being aware that you might be boring the other person with your conversation is not going to help with social relationships, if you still talk at length on the subject. This is the consciously incompetent state. I recall many times saying something like, 'I hope I'm not boring you by talking about…', but then carrying on talking anyway. The move from unconsciously incompetent to consciously competent with respect to social skills can be a very slow process of learning through repeated failure. I see now that I acquired better social understanding by experimenting with different social rules. I was not conscious of this at the time, but this is what I was doing. I have already mentioned one social rule that I developed, namely to avoid talking for too long on any one subject that might not be of interest to the other person.

Dr Temple Grandin and Sean Barron have written a book on the subject of rules of social relationships (Grandin and Barron 2005). In this book they describe ten rules of social relationships. The first rule states the most important point that social rules are not absolute. When I read these rules recently, I was immediately drawn to Rule 5, 'Being polite is appropriate in any situation'. I realized that this had been key to my increasing success in making friends. I learned that listening and asking the right questions to show an interest in the other person was a great way to make new friends. I continue to develop and refine my social rules based on how successful they have been when practised. I would like to provide a much more complicated rule that I use when I am faced with a friend who has a problem and is upset. My natural reaction is to immediately try to solve the problem by giving advice. This is often quite inappropriate. I think this is common behaviour with AS people. My rule in this situation is as follows:

1. Listen attentively and express an appropriate level of sympathy (e.g. nod and hold eye contact, concentrate on appropriate facial expression of concern).

2. Acknowledge and affirm the expressed feelings ('I see/hear/appreciate/understand that you're [expressed feeling], because…').

3. Share a related example from your own life, if you judge it to be helpful in illuminating the situation.

4. Offer a possible solution compassionately, explaining how it might help.

It is difficult to know when to move between these strategies, but in general people do not spend enough time in (1) and (2). There is a preference to move to (4) far too quickly.

My vision for the future in helping AS people develop social skills is to allow them to practise these skills in a safe, supportive environment. You could imagine a session that has as its objective to develop the ability to better help someone who is upset, because of a problem in their life. The session might involve some videoed role play where one person talks about the problem and the other person tries to be supportive in helping the person with this problem. A facilitator would observe the role play and manage a discussion afterwards that might involve playing back the video recording. This debrief might involve asking questions such as, 'How did that make you feel?' and 'What could you have done differently at that point?' It would be hoped that the two people involved in the role play would also learn from each other. I am convinced that I would have benefited greatly from such training and coaching as a child and as an adult.

I can converse with neurotypical people for several hours without too much difficulty. If I have to talk for much longer than this, I find that I get tired mentally. I know the signs for this now, and I try to find an excuse to leave the conversation or the group.

I can identify with the following extract from an online magazine article:

> At one end of the spectrum are people who retreat into their own world...at the other are those with 'high-functioning autism' who, though they lack some degree of intuition about what others are thinking, can often figure things out through logical analysis, a 'human-hacking' process not unlike the efforts of Mr. Spock, the half-human, half-Vulcan character in the TV series 'Star Trek'. (Ross 2006))

I have disclosed my AS diagnosis to one close friend who is female. She tells me that she would never know that I had AS from my behaviour. I think that I may be able to pass as normal in many everyday social situations because I've learned to figure out how to behave through logical analysis (the 'human-hacking' process). Perhaps my above-average IQ and the encouragement to learn that has been passed on to me by my parents has helped me work out how best to behave in most social situations, which in turn has increased my confidence in these situations. I should add that I have not yet been successful in intimate social relationships.

It does frustrate me that the price of this attempt to fit in is high levels of anxiety and stress and difficulties sleeping. It also irritates me that because I act normal, people think I must be normal and my inability to be successful in relationships must be due to me not trying hard enough or some other weakness of personality.

One of the reasons that I attribute to my poor ability to keep friends is the difficulty that I seem to have in knowing how I feel about the other person. I can enjoy time with the person, but then not remember this enjoyable emotional state afterwards. This means that the person can easily slip from my consciousness. I need to actively think about the person to keep them in my mind when I am not with them. I often seem to lack the motivation to do this enough, and this is not helped by the fact that I have poor visualization skills. I do have some practical strategies to help me remember other people in my life. I have put all my family and friends' birthdays in the Calendar function of Microsoft Outlook, which then automatically reminds me when there is a birthday due. I leave notes in conspicuous places around the house to remind me to contact someone I have not contacted for a while. I will send a card or flowers to someone who is unwell. In these simple, practical ways I am now a little better at maintaining friendships. Of course if there was some magic cure for my lack of emotional awareness, then I would be the first in the queue to receive it.

I have been told that I can present a rather wooden expression, which I know does not help me in social situations. A simple exercise that has helped me create a more consistently friendly expression is to practise relaxing and softening my face in a mirror.

I am sometimes poor at evaluating how I should respond in difficult social situations, and this can lead to inappropriate communication and behaviour. I know I need to evaluate more at the emotional level. I do feel more able to ask for feedback these days, if I think I have said or done something inappropriate. I am learning to recognize when I might be about to say something inappropriate, and mentally test it by asking myself questions such as, 'Could what I'm about to say upset or annoy the person?'

I have discovered a useful exercise that is helping me to read body language better. It involves recording a TV soap episode and then playing it back without the sound. I try to determine the emotional state of the actors from the non-verbal cues. I use a small tape recorder for this. I then play back the soap with the sound and assess how well I have done in identifying the correct emotions. I have discovered that I am much better at spotting certain emotions, such as fear and anger.

I have learned that some uncertainty is necessary in any relationship, so I cannot always resolve uncertainty. However, I need to recognize when not doing or saying something leaves the other person with an unfair level of uncertainty. I know this requires clear and assertive communication. I have always struggled with conflict in relationships, and with being assertive. I think this is partly explained by my difficulty in managing my own emotions and those in others. I am afraid of the emotions that seem to rise to the surface in confrontational situations. I am rather a passive person, a common trait in people with AS. I would certainly benefit from some coaching in managing emotions and in assertive behaviour.

Bibliography

Grandin, T. and Barron, S. (2005) *Unwritten Rules of Social Relationships: Decoding Social Mysteries through the Unique Perspective of Autism.* Arlington, TX: Future Horizons, Inc.

Ross, P. E. (2006) 'When Engineers' Genes Collide. IEEE Spectrum Online. Available at http://spectrum.ieee.org/oct0614665. Accessed 27 February 2007.

Chapter 3: The Difficulty of Social Contact and the Impact on My Mental Health

Hazel D.L. Pottage

Introduction by Luke Beardon
There is so much that could be noted about this powerful chapter; however, I think it is best to let it speak for itself. A superb account of what is, frighteningly and sadly, not a unique experience.

No one can make up for the lost years of misunderstanding and of the subsequent loneliness before a diagnosis of Asperger Syndrome and, believe me, being misunderstood has caused me much heartache and despair, the side effects being an addiction to food and to a lesser degree an addiction to alcohol.

Always being on the outside looking in on people but never feeling a part of what is going on must be the loneliest place on the planet.

Nowadays the thought that I would always have under my belt up to four large glasses of Baileys before entering a social situation fills me with horror.

After diagnosis I guess that I am left with a feeling of total confusion about even trying to understand neurotypical behaviour but I do understand myself much better and I now do not make the mistakes that I used to make in the past, such as diving into a group of people in the middle of a conversation and trying to join in. I now have got more used to people-watching and trying to assess when and where it is appropriate to enter a group of people and when it is not. I have also learned that it's OK to sit on the sidelines and watch and try to learn social cues and habits as this does not come at all naturally to me.

Sometimes I have found that when I sit back and relax and don't try and force myself on others they actually come and start a conversation with me for a short time before moving onto someone else.

Throughout my life I have had difficulties in keeping friendships. At school I had two female friends who took me under their wings; one when I first started school when I was lonely, confused, anxious and afraid, although she, too, was anxious and afraid but she had a more outgoing personality than me and she would come and sit next to me in class and she would stay with me during the school breaks. I liked her but at times she overwhelmed me because of her need to, I think, be in total control in the relationship and my quiet defensiveness.

During this time I was so deeply troubled but had no emotional way to express myself. Instead it came out in physical illnesses; this included the usual childhood illnesses but also at various stages all of the skin would peel off the palms of my hands and the soles of my feet. No doctor at the time could explain this other than it was down to severe emotional stress.

I changed schools and the physical illnesses stopped. However I lost my friend and was now left alone; it was a village school and to begin with my classmates seemed friendly – until the bullying started. I was bullied severely throughout my life in both junior school and senior school.

I did find some acquaintances at junior school, but looking back on it they just used me; they would show some superficial friendship then would talk about me behind my back and in the end they used to just talk about me to my face; I took it because they were the only friends that I had and I did not know how to make friends at playtime. Everyone was in their own groups of friends and there was me on my own; eventually, with the help of a rubber ball, I retreated into my own world because it was safer there. I could hear their name-calling but could carry on being in my own world with my ball, longing for home time and to be with my greatest friend, who was called Rufus – he was a large Golden Labrador dog – until the break period was over.

In class I could not keep up with most of the lessons and the teachers had to go slowly in order for me to catch up, much to the annoyance of my classmates.

A kind teacher arranged for a doctor to come into the school to assess me for dyslexia as I did mirror writing and no one could read it. But he told her I was lazy and said that she should give me more work to do.

I struggled on through my junior school. When I was 11, my parents found me a private tutor to teach me to write with the one-to-one tuition; with a good relationship with my tutor I came on more than I ever had done in the past and could write before I went to secondary school in at least a legible fashion.

But due to the years of isolation the unravelling of me as a person had begun. And the obsessions had started; I became obsessed with the lead singer of a 1970s rock band whose music I listened to constantly and I never stopped talking about him either.

By the age of 14 I was admitted to West End Adolescent Unit in 1976 where I spent three years of my life until 1979. I was so ill that I did not speak for about six months of my life and had to be washed and dressed by my mother for about a year.

I was completely obsessed with the lead singer of a 1970s boy band by now and thought I had powers to communicate with him telepathically and that I held his soul in my hand. I was told at the time that I suffered from severe anxiety and depression; I question this diagnosis to this day.

One day I would like to write about my experiences in the adolescent unit; however, until recently it has been too painful to even think about, although I have vivid memories of the place and the friendships that I made, especially with the other inmates. On one occasion when I was refusing to open my hands the staff denied me food; the others gathered around me and told me that they would get food to me and that they would refuse to see me starve.

I was also told that they could not figure out what was wrong with me. I think they were putting me somewhere between OCD and schizophrenia but they could not figure me out at all. However this did not stop them wanting to give me ECT when I was 14 and but for my father, who was clever enough to challenge them, God only knows where I would be today.

I guess the question could be asked: was I sane or was I crazy?

I left the adolescent unit at the age of 17 and with a renewed sense of enthusiasm re-entered the world. I went back to school into the sixth form to try and catch up on my education only to enter another very lonely and dark place. None of the sixth-form girls understood me nor I them. Again I was alone; they were bitchy, catty and cruel.

By the time I was in my twenties I was back under a psychiatrist and having another mental breakdown. He was a merciless and cruel man (plus he was very manipulative of my mother) who believed that he could help me. My father, however, saw through him and told me that he had failed me. This guy swallowed up any self-esteem that I had and told the world that I was severely disabled and that I was unemployable. He also made me believe that I was stupid. He did not understand the severe meltdowns that I was having at this time and more or less told me to pull myself together. Again, he did not know what was wrong with me; he suspected that it was possible brain damage that was organic in origin and that it had occurred at the time of my birth.

For many years I drifted, using mental health services on and off although I have to say that I still managed to accomplish quite a lot. I joined both Mind and the Red Cross with my mother: it was her way of trying to get me to socialize. I slowly began to rebuild my self-esteem and myself.

I had a personal break-through when I rediscovered my relationship with animals, and despite having a major setback when my father died ten years ago I attended agricultural college and received an NVQ qualification in animal husbandry.

My dream is to set up a community-based project where anyone can come and receive the kind of therapy I myself receive daily from animals. The other major break-through for me has been joining the mental health charity that I am currently a trustee of. It's been through the course of my work there and through meeting others with neurodiverse issues that I first went for a diagnosis for dyspraxia and after that Asperger Syndrome.

For me this has answered fully that my issues are neurological in nature and that in themselves they are not mental health problems. However, the years of being misunderstood have led me to suffer from mental ill-health. Looking back on the time when I was severely ill, the most prominent feeling that comes out of this is loneliness that was severe enough to make me mentally unwell.

My strategies now are to be very public about my Asperger Syndrome and not to feel the need to apologize if my behaviour is odd to neurotypical people, not to feel guilt and shame whenever I wish to be alone because a social situation is too much for me to handle, and to campaign to achieve better services for Asperger Syndrome and other neurodiverse issues and a better and richer understanding of them. My hope is that there will be better support/enablement/understanding for future generations.

Chapter 4: Social Relationships for People with Asperger Syndrome: How to Help People Understand

Giles Harvey

Introduction by Luke Beardon

Giles makes some pertinent points in this chapter, two of which are useful to highlight. The first regards the importance of trust when it comes to relationships – and the effect having a lack of trust can have on any given individual. As I noted in the introductory chapter I feel that this is one of the most important aspects of any relationship, and yet one of the most difficult to 'get right'. I have found it very useful, in my friendships with people with AS, to set out with my friends clear rules regarding expectations: For example, how often is OK to phone or email (obviously this is a two-way process). This introduces the notion of explicit trust, as opposed to implicit trust. Most NTs do not overtly discuss many aspects of a relationship that a person with AS requires in order to be successful. Being open and explicitly honest and proactive can be hugely beneficial. For example, saying that I will always read emails but will not have time to reply straight away to them means that both parties understand the 'rules' and thus have expectations that should be fulfilled. The idea of a 'contract' may sound somewhat over-formal – particularly to an NT – but if it strengthens the friendship there is no way it can be seen as a bad thing. At the very least it allows both individuals to state explicitly what they want out of the relationship, and individuals can come to a mutually acceptable agreement; this can obviously be changed as long as both people agree to the changes.

Giles also comments on the Government – and possible ways forward. I agree totally that those in power should recognize that providing appropriate social support (at any age) could have a huge and positive impact on those with AS. Not only would costs be hypothetically reduced in the long term (e.g. crisis intervention, psychiatric input, the penal system, benefits) but the overall humanitarian improvements would be priceless.

I was trying to recapture my youth a few weeks ago by visiting one of the websites which gives information about the Australian soap opera *Neighbours*, and a thought came to me, that often I am like a long-serving character: everyone stays a short time and leaves and I am left alone. What do I mean? Well quite often during the course of my life there have been people I would have liked to have known better but I didn't know how to strike up a proper friendship with them. When life has changed, which it often does, through work and education, they have moved on to bigger and better things while I have been left behind, never to see them again. I wonder, quite often, what they are doing.

I have always struggled to find friendships which have been lasting. People would simply walk away, as they couldn't understand my body language, and perhaps thought me a bit rude or ignorant. I might have said the wrong thing, perhaps something inappropriate without thinking, or they haven't wanted to know me because I don't follow the latest fashions in clothes, films and music. It may be because they consider my hobbies bizarre; hobbies like collecting bus memorabilia or street atlases or whatever. Quite often, also, I would talk about my hobbies until people were bored. I would hate to think how many people I put off for one of these reasons.

In later life I have probably been excluded from friendships, as I haven't held jobs down for long periods of time, especially in my initial years post-university. Then, perhaps, I ought to have been employed in a place with lots of young people itching for a night out. There have been the people I have put off when I have been depressed. Sometimes being depressed, and speaking negatively, may discourage people from making the effort to get to know someone.

However, when I say I have no friends, I am not being completely honest. I have a friend of a similar age who hasn't got a diagnosis of AS, but has another mild disability. We see each other at weekends, principally on Saturday nights, and until recently there was another non-AS friend without any disability, who has now drifted away when he met the girl of his dreams. We are still in occasional contact, as is another more distant friend. I like having this contact, as these friends don't know about Asperger Syndrome which means I can escape Asperger Syndrome for a bit. I have been friends with these people since college.

There are also people who I have met through Asperger Syndrome groups. Most of these are even more distant friends, as I tend to associate with them depending on employment commitments. Also, quite often, while not trying to be too big headed, I can feel more of a carer to them, as that was my original role when I was employed as such. Because I function well with my Asperger Syndrome, often people want advice on many different issues, so seeing me as a friend rather than a carer has been quite difficult for them to do.

There are other times, however, when I do not want to make social contact and much prefer my own space in my own surroundings. Perhaps this too, has put some people off me. I might go for a drive alone or go shopping alone, or even on holiday alone, and I am not worried travelling alone in the car to far away places.

So what might have helped?
Another way I have met people is through specialized interest groups. Again these are people that I have more distant friendships with as I don't tend to see them that often, perhaps monthly at meetings, but it could be more or less often depending on what it is I am doing.

No matter what hobby you have there are probably others with similar interests who will meet up to discuss their hobbies, or on the internet chat rooms. (Be careful not to give too much data on yourself away!) From sewing and lace, to trains and buses, to playing a musical instrument, whatever your interest there are no doubt all sorts of groups where like-minded people exist.

You may also meet people through holidays.

An earlier diagnosis might have meant people in my earlier years may have understood more and perhaps have been more supportive of my needs. From that, maybe, I might have made some additional friends – who knows?

Perhaps an earlier introduction, from earlier diagnosis to treatment, might also have worked. Many professionals who work with people with Asperger Syndrome believe social skills workshops or circle groups help. These work in the following way: people with Asperger Syndrome and high-functioning autism discuss social issues and how to behave appropriately in a wide variety of social situations.

I was fortunate to be able to partake in a social group for a short time in my early twenties and we all picked up useful social skills by exchanging ideas and information about how to react appropriately, rules about spacing in crowds and other such skills. Unfortunately social skills workshops or circle groups are quite rare, as few people are trained to actually deliver them and also because there is no specific funding for them from local authorities and Government. It might help if Government and local authorities were to look at the wider view of such groups, in that by providing these they reduce long-term funding issues as people become more socially able, and therefore less socially isolated and consequently less likely to be depressed.

If I could have been persuaded, when younger, to try and do other things, even if they weren't easy, this may have introduced me to potential friends; for example, if I had been good at cycling I could have joined a cycling group, or good at playing a musical instrument I could have joined an orchestra. Maybe I would have met similar people. Unfortunately most hobbies taken up by people with Asperger Syndrome are the sort which can be and are largely done alone, so the opportunities to meet others are substantially reduced.

Perhaps another mistake I have made in the past, was there was always a desire, when at school and at college and university, to be involved with the in-crowd or the most popular people, and not those who perhaps weren't, for whatever reason. The people who are popular would probably never want someone like myself to cramp their style, and perhaps I might have done better to try to be with those who were less popular and therefore more likely to be like myself. The same ideology applies to sexual relationships, for like reasons.

Another way people with Asperger Syndrome can be encouraged to meet others is through employment. Employment offers a chance to meet others and in some circumstances fellow employees might become friends, because they share similar interests in things like music, sport or television. In order to achieve more opportunities through employment, more supported employment schemes for people with Asperger Syndrome need to be offered, but again quite often this is hampered in various areas by Government or local government funding criteria.

What mistakes can people with Asperger Syndrome make on the route to making friends?

Sometimes, some people with Asperger Syndrome can unfortunately be manipulated for all sorts of different reasons. People with Asperger Syndrome become very trusting, as they obviously want friends. People who haven't got the same interests at heart, from the school bully to the thief, to the paedophile or sex predator, can trick them into all sorts of difficult situations. Therefore it is important that we teach people with Asperger Syndrome that not all people are nice people and that they may not have the same intentions. They need to know how to spot if they are being taken advantage of; they should also know that friends can't be bought by lending compact discs, buying drinks or whatever else people with Asperger Syndrome might be manipulated into doing. Friendships need to be age appropriate, especially where children and adolescents are involved. *[Editors' note: many children with AS seem not to identify other people by age, and thus shun social interaction with peers, choosing instead to interact with adults. Sometimes this may be because of the high intellectual ability of the child with AS. While it is accepted that often social relationships are deemed more appropriate when ages are similar, the most important consideration is whether both individuals involved are happy and risk-free. We do not wish to suggest that age differences mean that a relationship is not warranted.]*

People with Asperger Syndrome may also think that a friendship doesn't involve two-way interaction; they might expect a friend to do all the giving and do all the compromising while they take all, so to speak. Of course this isn't the way friendships work. Quite often I have had to make sacrifices for friends or have done something with friends that I might not have wanted to do. Any good friends will of course repay this back in kind, to the extent of doing something which the person with Asperger Syndrome wishes to do. The same applies to using the telephone: if someone is making all the telephone calls perhaps they might get fed up and decide that they are just being taken advantage of. Social skills workshops ought to clarify the situation regarding compromising with others.

Another thing I have struggled with and found particularly difficult, is how to hold friendships or say the correct thing to people of the opposite sex. Issues for females are very different, and there are statements that put off or offend women. Highlighting women doing jobs or pastimes that were previously the dominance of men or where females are in a minority, suggesting that household chores are a woman's preserve or expressing different perspectives on issues surrounding sex, childbirth and intelligence, all need to be approached with care. Also I have had to become aware that females require their own space, such as groups for them alone and not for men. *[Editors' note: we do not wish to suggest in any way that gender equality be compromised, either within the population of individuals with AS or in an AS/NT relationship. However, we do accept that for someone with AS it can be very difficult to understand the needs of others – both male and female.]*

Women equally can't always understand men and men can be offended by certain sexual remarks that women may make, or may suffer feelings of inadequacy if they appear to be performing less well than the women that are around them.

What are the consequences of having Asperger Syndrome which has caused lack of friendships?

Well, quite simply, there are lots of major consequences. The biggest consequence has been bullying and loneliness in the school years which led to loneliness in adult life and in turn depression, partially as a result of being isolated.

Other problems have been the fact that it has become harder to find a girlfriend. Girlfriends obviously would usually start off as friends rather than sexual partners. Consequently, this has led to other problems, as I have never married and now that I am in my thirties doubt that I am ever likely to do so. This, in turn, means I have no children, and therefore, presumably will lack companionship in later life when it becomes harder to get about.

Another consequence which isn't quite as obvious is that it has made success in the jobs market all the harder. Many jobs are found by knowing others already working within a company and may never actually go to full interview process, or if they do there is a preference for a person the employer is already acquainted with, especially if it is known they can do the job.

It has probably also had an effect on other areas of my life by reducing confidence, giving me a fear of being criticized by others, and a feeling I cannot speak my own mind because of the fear of offending others. I feel it has denied me the opportunity to travel to far away places in the world. It has also probably caused other issues we don't think about like physical health problems caused through lack of exercise, through not having any need to go outside the house, due to social isolation.

Being bullied in childhood, because of having Asperger Syndrome has probably made it harder for me to trust others and therefore harder to make new friends.

In conclusion, I would state it is true to say that friendships are very important to everybody's well-being; without friendships we lack access to so many other different areas of life.

Other friends

Other friends do exist if the person with Asperger Syndrome has a supportive family unit. I come from a very small family unit because neither my mother or father had any brothers or sisters and therefore I have no cousins, uncles and aunts. So you can see how additional friends might exist in a family unit. My father, mother and brother have all been very loyal and supportive to me throughout my life, and therefore I see them as friends like any other type of friend, as well as parents and brother.

What might happen in the future?

Who knows what the Government may introduce to support people who have Asperger Syndrome to find friends? Certainly there is the possibility that social skills training might reduce longer-term costs in health care, which arise due to problems that are quite often caused by lack of access to friendships and by isolation. Social skills workshops might also allow people with Asperger Syndrome to gain the necessary skills to survive in the workplace. Therefore social skills workshops at the earliest available opportunity might provide cost-effective solutions to reducing the longer-term costs incurred by mental health problems, developed as a secondary feature to Asperger Syndrome as a result of having no social contact.

What cannot happen, and I wouldn't expect to happen, is for people to go out to find friends for me, as obviously friendships cannot be influenced by other people.

I would hope that one day the Government would take a longer-term view of what might be more cost-effective for people with Asperger Syndrome, rather than a political view, which decides that they won't be in government long term so why not pass on the problem for the next government and so on. The taxpayer continues to carry the burden and nothing constructive is done, but who knows?

I also wonder what other methods could be put into place to help people with Asperger Syndrome survive life with adequate friendships to offer support. Some solutions might come from technology. Already software exists to teach people with autism and Asperger Syndrome to understand facial expressions, but perhaps in the future computer software might similarly be developed to help people with a diagnosis of Asperger Syndrome to interact in different situations much more fully than just showing how to read facial expressions. For example, if it allowed you to actually speak to others, and imaginary people online react to what's actually being said to them, it could judge different situations and tell you why the imaginary people have reacted in the way they have done, which would be extremely beneficial to someone with Asperger Syndrome. However, it would take a lot of manpower hours and time to get a system which was so sophisticated to cover all the more likely possibilities, as not everyone is the same, and people can act differently based upon how they actually feel in themselves. Therefore it might be expensive or prohibitive cost-wise, and I might be inclined to question how practical such a solution might be.

In my own case I do not know what the likely outcome from tomorrow will be with friends and relationships: it depends on who I meet on life's journey, what I can cope with myself, and what the people I meet actually want from me and if they feel comfortable around me.

Chapter 5: Social Relationships and the Communication Problem

Neil Shepherd

Introduction by Luke Beardon

This is a great chapter to read for anyone who still needs convincing that people with AS do have a sense of humour. It used to be the case that so-called professionals would aver that people with AS lacked a sense of humour, but if you spend time with individuals you will see time and time again that this is simply not the case. I suspect what people actually meant was that individuals with AS may not share the same sense of humour as most NTs – but, it has to be said, so what? The humour of the person with AS is often different, sometimes (to me) a little surreal – but perfectly evident. In fact, I think that many individuals with AS find things funny that would never even occur to most NTs – and, thus, have access to a whole new world of humour. To not recognize this is a great injustice to a population that has so much to give. It is interesting that Neil communicates his perspectives in such an effective way – and this is someone who is labelled as impaired in communication. Both the humour aspect and the communication aspect highlight one of the fundamental problems in society – NTs suggesting lack of humour and impaired communication simply because people with AS do not share the same humour nor exactly the same communication as NTs. Surely it is obvious that this is ethically and morally wrong.

Introduction

They say that the measure of a man is shown by the quality of the friends that he keeps. If this is the case then I don't actually exist (in which case, how are you reading this?). You see, I don't have friends. Yes I know people, yes I have acquaintances and colleagues, and yes I talk to people (sometimes)…but I don't have 'friends'. I've never had 'friends'. In fact, what is a 'friend'?

At the core of the Asperger 'problem' is an inability to communicate – it's a communication problem after all and nowhere is this issue more prominent than in social relationships and social interaction. Aspergic people are often stereotyped as being 'loners' but is this a fair label to apply? I suppose we'd best look at the problem and see what lessons and observations pop out of the pea that I use in place of a brain.

The need for friends

Man, irrespective of any 'problems', is primarily a social animal and needs contact with other people. Social interaction is vital to mental well-being and key to not going insane (when looked at in a very simplistic way). Is there a difference, though, between 'people' and 'friends'? The answer is a resounding 'yes'. We all know people but how many of the people that you know would you consider to be a friend? Is your bank manager a friend? Is your postman a friend? In the case of your postman you, more than likely, see them every day but, unless your postman actually *is* someone whom you spend time with, they're not normally someone whom you can talk to, open up to and let into your most inner thoughts and feelings.

A 'friend', by my own definition of the term, is someone who may share a common interest, someone whom you feel comfortable discussing your innermost thoughts and feelings with, someone whose company you actually enjoy. This is massively different to an acquaintance or colleague, who, to a certain degree, you have to almost tolerate – fate has thrown this person at you (possibly through a work situation) and the pair of you *have* to communicate but this communication comes about because of a practical need and not necessarily through any great desire to understand or offer genuine support to each other. In my job I often have to speak to people (either face to face or through media such as email or telephone) but it's because of a need to exchange information so that I can get my job done (or so that they can get their job done) – there's almost no 'non-vital' information exchange.

Aspergic people need to deal with people too and have just as much a need for 'friends' as anyone else. The problem, though, because of the inherent communication difficulties, soon becomes blatantly obvious. So much of human interaction is done on a subconscious level often via implied meanings and systems such as body language. The Aspergic mind though has great difficulties with these things and in an uninformed society, their actions are very often misunderstood or misinterpreted.

A couple of girls – misinterpretation and misunderstood

James Whale's 1935 horror classic *The Bride of Frankenstein* (trust me, this is going somewhere) is a very good analogy to the problems that Aspergic people face when it comes to social relationships. In the film the monster (Boris Karloff) comes to the conclusion that he is lonely so sets out to find a friend (and ultimately a bride) (this is in stark contrast to the earlier 1931 Frankenstein when he was only interested in killing people – if he was truly Aspergic then he'd probably feel like killing people quite often...I know I certainly do). *[Editors' note: we do not suggest in any way that this should be taken literally – people with AS are generally not aggressive or wishing to harm others. We do recognize, however, that the pain experienced by people with AS living in the NT world can induce feelings which are extreme and sometimes difficult to cope with.]* Even though he has acquaintances in the shape of Baron Frankenstein (Colin Clive) and Dr Praetorius (Ernest Thesinger) he has the need for a 'friend' – someone that he trusts, someone who he feels comfortable with and someone that he wants to spend time with for a purely 'enjoyable' reason. As the film progresses we see his stumbling attempts to find this 'friend' and repeatedly see the way that society misinterprets his actions. To the young shepherdess he is a lumbering brute, to the two hunters he's 'the fiend who's been terrorizing half the countryside'. Only in the blind hermit does he discover someone who sees past the exterior and discovers the person inside.

Karloff's plight actually gives us an insight into how the world, to a certain degree, responds and behaves to the Aspergic person. Although to me (just as with the monster) my actions are perfectly sensible, to others they are very often misunderstood and misinterpreted, and because I don't conform to the social 'normals' many people find that difficult to handle.

The daily ritual of saying 'Good morning', for example, serves no practical purpose but failing to respond to this pointless statement marks one as being 'ignorant'. The same goes with the classic statement 'Lovely weather'. What *is* the correct response to this statement? Society dictates that this should be the opening to a conversation that will encompass everything from last night's soap operas to the state of the nation and whether or not the local football team will get hammered at the weekend. How can this be? It's not logical. 'Lovely weather' is not the start to a conversation. It's a statement, a fact (possibly in error as I look out of the window on a cold November afternoon) and has about as much 'conversation' potential as stating that the sky is blue or that post boxes are red. I'm diverging but I am demonstrating the logical mindset of the Aspergic mind. Non-Aspergics, though, don't expect this purely logical outlook and when they don't get the 'correct' response, it makes them feel very uncomfortable.

As animals we soon learn that if something tastes bad or hurts, we don't eat it or do it. The same is true, to a certain degree, of conversation and being made to feel uncomfortable – if a particular person makes you feel uncomfortable or doesn't respond in the way that you want/need then you tend to avoid them if you can (for example just think of the times that you have to deal with a known awkward customer/client – it's a chore and not something to relish). Talking to and communicating with Aspergic people is often hard work and people have to adjust their expectations and, for a change, have to think about what's being said (as they're not always going to get the 'expected' response) or modify how they express themselves. This, though, is more difficult than just talking to John from Accounts so I'll just go and see him instead.

The unwritten rules

This concept of 'being comfortable' extends beyond what is actually being physically said though and also impacts on the subconscious forms of communication. The accepted normal of holding eye contact, maintaining interest etc., doesn't always take place in the Aspergic mind. Eye contact can be fleeting (or non-existent, or, in some cases, extreme to the point of staring) and, as this isn't the 'expected' response/behaviour, it is easily misinterpreted. It's certainly not intentional but it makes the other party feel uncomfortable and gives people another 'excuse' for not wanting to talk to the Aspergic person. Body language also comes into this and, just as non-Aspergics give out body language that isn't recognized or understood, so too do Aspergics often give out the incorrect body language. I myself often adopt a very aggressive stance and have been told that I come across as being confrontational – I don't mean to but it just happens and I have no control over it. Again this works against social interaction as non-Aspergics feel uncomfortable, threatened etc., and it's another reason to avoid that person.

To a certain degree conversations often follow a 'script' – person A says X so person B says Y. This is fine and often very understandable. In my head (I can't speak for other Aspergics on this one) I stick to this formula fairly rigidly and expect that if I say A then the other person will say B, I'll then say C and they'll then say D. I prepare the conversation beforehand and it makes sense as I'll get the information across and get back the information that I need. The problem is, I'm Aspergic and I think in Aspergic terms rather than non-Aspergic terms so I never do manage to get it right. What typically happens to my beautifully rehearsed scenario is that I say A, the other person says Z…and I'm lost and baffled.

From a certain perspective it could be said that it's not so much what you say but how you say it (to a certain degree): the subconscious messages that your body gives off and whether or not you stick to the prescribed 'rules'. Aspergics often face other problems with communication, though, and this is down to what they're actually saying. Sometimes I consider Asperger Syndrome to be 'the honesty disease' as Aspergics are often totally frank and honest…sometimes brutally so. Having a lack of emotional understanding, it's very difficult to grasp how a piece of information or an action will be received or interpreted. The concept of 'sugar coating' just doesn't ever occur. This isn't down to Aspergic people being cruel or deliberately nasty but comes back to not understanding or realizing that an action will result in particular response/reaction.

A classic example of this happened to me once when I had to create a new password for a user. I chose a password based on the information to hand (I won't say what the actual word was but I'd been hassled repeatedly about getting this sorted out so it kind of followed along those kind of lines). Let's just say that the response wasn't 'positive'. I hadn't set out to cause offence and had approached the situation from a totally logical point of view but, being unable to understand the emotional elements involved, had managed to upset the person enormously. When it was pointed out I understood, but the lack of emotional understanding had caused this situation to arise. Why am I blabbering on about this? Well, partly to demonstrate this concept of 'expectation' (i.e. things to be 'sugar coated' as opposed to brutally honest) but it also shows what happens when an almost emotionless person has to deal with an emotional person. *[Editors' note: people with AS are not generally emotionless – it is emotional understanding that often cause problems, rather than a lack of emotions themselves.]* Neither understands each other and the misunderstanding can often result in a great deal of negativity and a breakdown in communication, and these types of situations almost always quickly spiral out of control.

Society dictates that we behave in a particular way and that we should follow certain rules and etiquette, wording things and approaching situations in almost a set manner. The Aspergic mind, having failed to recognize or understand these 'unwritten rules' (or the resultant responses) often comes across as being rude, ignorant, nasty or just outright cruel. My father (a suspected Aspergic) would often pass brutally frank judgement on what people wore directly to them (much to my mother's embarrassment). He wasn't setting out to be rude or nasty but 'I can't believe you wore that shirt' was just his way of expressing what he thought and he'd say it as bluntly as that rather than sugar coat it. A lot of people misinterpret this kind of 'honesty', failing to realize that what is actually being said is (probably) true. Many Aspergics are described as being tactless and it's not down to nastiness but down to being 'honest' – a fact that many non-Aspergics fail to understand.

From personal experience, as a child I was always regarded as the 'master of tact-less' and, in a desire to 'conform', I quickly realized that, just as with things that tasted bad or things that hurt when you touched them, saying X would result in a slap (I had cruel, cruel parents)...so I stopped doing it. As an adult I *should* be able to identify what will/won't cause offence but, possibly because of being Aspergic, I can't. As that child though, being unable to work out what resulted in 'pain' (either the physical as administered by my parents or exclusion/derision as later administered by peers) led to not saying anything – very much the old adage 'If you can't say anything good, don't say anything at all'. The habits learned in childhood though often carry through into adulthood and, although now more aware of other people (insomuch as I understand that they don't all have my twisted sense of humour or that they have stupid elements such as 'emotions', rather than understanding the exact elements that will cause offence) this adherance to the 'If you can't say anything...' adage persists, with the result being that I very often don't say anything lest I upset someone else. Is this true for all Aspergics? I hope not but I do wonder just how many other adult Aspergics have 'learned' that doing this is a way of avoiding immediate pain (despite the amount of psychological damage that it can do to 'bottle things up').

Being unable to understand other people's emotional needs and responses also is a big problem for Aspergics but there are others, with the final significant one being the inability to deal with conversation once it has started. This is not the case of actually trying to start conversation but rather the failure to identify when the other party should be able to respond, when the conversation has reached its natural conclusion etc. Aspergics are often seen as 'rambling' or fixating and we can seem to come across as something of a stuck record, endlessly repeating the same information, keeping going long after the other party has lost all interest. Aspergics, being unable to identify the 'unwritten rules', fail to see that the other party isn't interested, has lost interest. It does work both ways though and I know that I very often fail to see points in conversations when it's my turn to speak – this appears to be a common feature in Aspergic people as we miss the subconscious 'cues' that say 'I've stopped speaking – your turn now'. As with so many other elements of social interaction, it's another factor, another instance of making people uncomfortable (and encouraging their subsequent 'retreat') and another barrier.

Manifestations

It's obvious that there's a great deal of misinterpretation and misunderstanding going on (in both the Aspergic and non-Aspergic approach to communication) but what effect does this have on Aspergic people and why is it even a problem? As mentioned above, Aspergic people need human contact just as much as anyone else, but society's misinterpretation of the Aspergic 'way' (when it comes to communication) means that it's all too easy to become shunned and isolated – Neil doesn't behave 'normally' so I'd rather not bother. That's brutal and simplistic but is, fundamentally, the problem that a lot of Aspergics find themselves faced with (the not bothering that is, not being called 'Neil' – this is a problem in it's own right, though, as some smart Alec will *always* make the 'hilarious' joke of kneeling when introduced to me. Oh how we laugh and then I beat them to a bloody pulp with a handy piece of office furniture).

Being unable to find people who understand or are tolerant enough to handle the 'quirks' of interacting with Aspergics can quickly and easily lead to isolation and, naturally, depression. This is very much a result of basic human nature (almost 'dislike of the unlike') but overcoming the problem is not an easy one when certain other common Aspergic 'traits' are taken into account. It's all too easy for Aspergics to push society away but getting back comes with extra 'problems'.

Right under their noses

Given all of the difficulties associated with communicating with Aspergic people, why should non-Aspergics ever try to get past the initial 'barriers' and bother trying to befriend someone in this position? Contrary to popular belief, Aspergic people are not insane (often they have a skewed perspective of the world but they're not insane) and their brains, although different, do actually work. The honesty that can prove to be too great for some people to handle means that Aspergic people can often provide a very fresh and different viewpoint to the rest of the world (that's not to say that Aspergics are always honest but…). This alternative view of the world also often provides a counterbalance to other conventional views (and can be very useful in certain situations) – it's a chance to see how a different type of brain interprets things…and you can usually guarantee that it's picked out things that non-Aspergics have missed (as well as having missed the blatantly 'obvious' – this in itself often forces people to have to explain things and, as a consequence, better understand and analyse what it is that they're trying to say).

What often comes as a surprise to many people is that 'the quiet guy in the corner' actually *wants* to talk but, for reasons that we'll come on to later, can't. Anyone who can get into that little world often discovers a mine of information, an intelligent brain that is refreshingly different from the 'normal'. The biggest shock to many people, especially in my case, is that this 'enigma' is actually able to exhibit skills and abilities that they never realized they possessed…the most obvious and usual one being humour. Many descriptions of Asperger Syndrome state that Aspergics don't understand humour and this often interpreted literally as meaning that Aspergics don't have a sense of humour at all. Oh but we do, even if it does tend to leave a lot of people baffled (or maybe that's just my twisted sense of what's funny).

Far from being the emotional blocks of ice that people initially perceive, Aspergics are just as fully formed and developed as non-Aspergics, but the difficulties brought about by the nature of the condition mean that getting at the person 'inside' is often very difficult (and from the 'inside' it's very difficult to get 'out' and break people's initial perception).

Forming, or trying to form, a relationship with an Aspergic person isn't easy and there are a lot of adjustments that have to be made and allowed for. The social 'protocols' are often lacking or non-existent, the 'hidden cues' (in both conversational structure/timing and actual information) are often missed, and topics of conversation are often 'different' or 'restricted' (just think about the 'lovely weather' situation – this is not a topic, it's a statement and random statements don't, logically, lead to a conversation). Often a topic may not be of interest but, rather than feign interest (as a person is generally expected to do), an Aspergic person will be brutally honest and just not be interested. This is not done through selfishness or malice but because the person is genuinely not interested and is not constrained by 'etiquette'. There are also other factors that apply to some Aspergics and not to others. In my case, group situations make me uncomfortable and the more people involved in a conversation, the more I withdraw – one to one I'm fine, but as more people are introduced into a conversation, the more I'll withdraw and the less I'll say (this could be due to being overly self-conscious or having difficulty tracking more than one conversation at a time – it descends into one generic 'noise' rather than distinctive conversation). Factors like this often dictate how and when Aspergics will and won't engage in conversation and understanding that a person is being 'quiet' or failing to engage because of the nature of AS, rather than through ignorance (for example), is key to forming a relationship with an Aspergic.

It's definitely worth the effort, though, and anyone who can make the 'adjustments' and has the necessary understanding will often find a delicate little flower of a person who, for whatever reason (self-defence, protection, ignorance of others etc.), has positioned him/herself behind a ten-foot concrete wall. Many people who've made the effort with me are genuinely surprised by what they find. Instead of the monosyllabic 'iceman' is someone who is funny, intelligent, knowledgeable and thoughtful and is capable of providing interesting conversation and an encyclopaedic knowledge (of some subjects anyway) (I should probably say modest too).

The invisible wall

I've detailed why it's important to have 'friends', what the necessary adjustments are that need to be made (by non-Aspergics), and why many non-Aspergics often fail to understand certain actions and responses given by Aspergics, but what stops Aspergic people from being able to talk, approach social situations etc.?

When my diagnosis was revealed to the world (i.e. work) the stock response was 'Oh, if you're having a problem, just come and talk to me'. How? To a non-Aspergic this would just be a case of going up to the person and talking to them. For someone who doesn't understand, or has a limited understanding of, social skills this is a very daunting task. Especially in adult Aspergics, you're very much aware of elements of social interaction of which you have no understanding (you know that they're there but you just don't know how they work – like the insides of your PC or a woman's head). This is often not a conscious thought process and somewhere in the brain warning flags are popping up and alarm bells are ringing as you're having to deal with a situation that you have little or no control over. You get nervous (actually most people get nervous but in Aspergics the nervousness is somehow amplified) and, just as with a pain or something that tastes bad, you (often subconsciously and automatically) avoid that situation or environment. If that situation is 'talking' then you don't talk as 'talking' equals 'pain' (in a stress sense, not in an arm-twisted-behind-your-back sense).

This automatic response is something that most people fail to understand and they can't grasp that something as simple as 'talking' can produce such an extreme reaction at a subconscious level. Can it be overcome? In simple terms yes but from my experiences so much effort goes into controlling the fear and 'pain' (or rather *hiding* the fear and pain) that you don't actually have enough processing power left to hold the conversation, understand what's being said or form rational responses. With social interaction being such a core element of the human condition, anyone who lacks that element has great difficulty explaining the problem. Conversely, it becomes very difficult to understand how someone could be missing this ability – it's never given conscious thought, so 99 per cent of people fail to realize the thought processes that *are* going on or fully understand what they're actually doing.

Round and round in circles

With this 'invisible wall' around them Aspergics immediately face a problem when it comes to going out and making friends (rather than have people come to them – it just doesn't happen by the way). There's an obvious need for friends and human interaction, but is it worth the effort and how do you solve the problem?

From bitter experience I can say that having social contact is far, far preferable to not having social contact. This doesn't mean that I actually have social contact but that I know that life is pretty miserable without it. At several stages in my life I've become isolated (through having to move to a new area, the departure of a spouse, etc.) and it's at times like these that people either sink or swim, metaphorically speaking (or maybe literally speaking if you've just taken a new job on an oil rig and it collapses into the sea) (note to self: never get job on oil rig).

Making social contact, finding friends etc., is not easy for anyone but it is far more difficult for anyone who deviates from 'normal', whether that be through AS or other conditions. Society is not geared up for 'non-normals' and through ignorance (not deliberate I would like to point out) is unaware of the problems, difficulties and extra consideration that have to be made for them. As an Aspergic person I think they *should* be more aware but, from a more pragmatic perspective, why should they be? 'Non-normals' make up a very small percentage of population and, as a civilization, we do tend to live by 'majority rule' (and at a basic level we also tend do adopt the 'dislike of the unlike' attitude).

The problem that faces anyone who is 'alone' is one of how to re-enter society – I'm stuck at home but how do I meet like-minded people when I don't know anyone? Where do I go to meet people? etc. Add into this a difficulty in being able to communicate with people and you have a situation where people are not only isolated but where they *know* that they are isolated but are unable to find a way to help themselves to get out of their particular 'hole'.

Many situations and scenarios involved with social contact typically revolve around an existing 'social circle' but breaking into such a system is not easy when you're the outsider looking in. In many senses you almost need to be 'invited' into the circle but here we hit an almost chicken-and-egg scenario – you don't know anyone so how do you get invited?

For Aspergic people, with their difficulties in communication, alternative 'needs' and heightened sense of self-consciousness, making that initial contact can be very difficult and stressful – you're typically entering an environment over which you have no control and of which you have possibly very little (or no) experience. Sometimes it works and, having managed to control/hide nervousness and appear 'normal', you can be accepted but other times it doesn't work and the results can not only be negative but they can also dent confidence etc.

Stand up...be counted

Meeting people and making social contact isn't easy for Aspergic people and a lot of the problems come down to ignorance about the condition (the first thought that always goes through my head is 'Do I mention AS or just keep schtum?') and the 'by definition' anxiety and stress that are generated as a result of simply being Aspergic and being placed in an 'unknown' situation.

Social relationships and interaction are difficult and I wish that I knew how to overcome these problems, where to meet people etc. Like so many aspects of AS though, perseverance is probably the only answer – the world won't come to you, you have to go and face the world...no matter how hard that might be, and hopefully you can find people who are smart enough to think beyond 'normal'. Even with over 6.5 billion people in it, if you don't go out there, the world can be a very lonely place.

Chapter 6: Social Relationships and Social Inclination

Alexandra Brown

Introduction by Luke Beardon

All of what Alex has to say is fascinating; one particular aspect I think is worth highlighting. I believe that there is a distinct difference between an intellectual understanding of a problem and the emotional response to it. Just because someone has an understanding, for example, of why a particular situation might occur, it does not mean that they are automatically going to be able to cope with it on an emotional level. NTs are not that dissimilar – you may understand why your partner has run off with someone else, but it does not reduce the hurt in any way. I think the difference between NTs and those with AS in this area is the lack of empathy – not of people with AS, but of NTs. It is common for NTs to point out the environmental processes that have led to a problem, and then make the assumption that all will then be OK. For example, explaining that there is a reason for being late and assuming that that then marks the end of the problem. Just knowing why something has happened does not change the feelings that an individual might have. So, it is not good enough simply to explain why something has happened without fully taking into account the emotional response that the environmental factors have elicited. It may well be that it is difficult or impossible to reduce stress and anxiety once a situation has occurred, but at least acknowledging it is a good starting point.

I think when I was younger I would have described myself as being anti-social, but that's not really what I meant, and I have latterly arrived at the term 'unsociable'. There was a time when I wanted to be sociable, in particular during my teenage years and early twenties; but it's not the case any more. At one point I may have felt sad thinking this, but now I am quite happy about it. I think it was more a case of expectations placed on me by other people, or wanting to appear to fit in that made me feel that I had to try to make friends and go out and socialize.

Personally I find any social occasion to be an extremely stressful experience. People seem to be so unpredictable, and even more so if they have been drinking, and I tend to feel totally out of my depth. The problem is, that other people seem to expect you to attend certain events, and even think that you would like to do so and will find it an enjoyable experience. There is also an expectation on you to join in with conversation, in which you may have no interest and nothing to contribute. In terms of conversation generally, first, it's very hard to think of anything to say in the first place, although if you know you have a common interest that may help. Second, it can be difficult to concentrate if the conversation is based purely on social chit chat, or a subject outside your experience. On these occasions, I tend to drift off or feel extremely uncomfortable. I often think about something in my head, which may or may not be related to the topic of conversation, and then say something about it, not realizing that the other person has no idea what I am talking about. Also, it is difficult to know when people have finished talking, and then I end up accidentally interrupting them. Sometimes I realize I have done it, and sometimes I don't. When I am observing a conversation, I sometimes think of something relevant to say, but there seems to be no point where I can join in; or the subject changes and I don't know whether it is still all right to say what I was going to say, or not to bother. I used to notice that when I took a break with work colleagues, I would often make a comment, and then everyone went quiet and it killed the conversation. I used to find this puzzling, but now I find it quite funny. Also, what are you supposed to do if someone or something interrupts the conversation? For example, if a child cries, obviously they can't be ignored, so should you carry on talking or wait until it's quiet again; and then is it OK to continue with the same subject because you don't know where the other person heard up to, or they may no longer be interested. Another difficulty is that sometimes you are expected to lie. I don't really like lying, and I don't find it easy. Sometimes though it seems like you need to in order not to hurt people's feelings. I think that is a bit different to lying and being deliberately deceitful. Or maybe it is better to always be totally honest. I usually try and avoid saying anything at all rather than risk upsetting someone.

I find that there are some people whom I can hold a conversation with. Sometimes I am interested in their hobbies or job, and can ask them questions about it, or we may have a common interest, or I can talk to people who either don't mind or are used to how I speak. In some instances it is a case of feeling comfortable with a person, and not feeling threatened or that they are going to humiliate you in some way. When I was younger I tried to join in with the other students at school and at college, sometimes I would forget what I was trying to say part way through, or I would be talking about something, and everyone would suddenly start talking over me and ignoring me. They would even do this as soon as I started talking. I quite often get an adrenalin rush when I have to talk to people, especially people I don't know, or in front of groups of people.

I think that one of the aspects that terrify me about social occasions, is if it is a situation I have not been in before or where I am uncertain what to do. It seems silly, because in some ways I have always felt proud to be different, particularly in circumstances where I feel secure, but something as simple as going out for a meal is a nightmare scenario for me. I don't understand how most people seem to know what to do when they go to a café or a restaurant. There seem to be no set rules. In some places you sit and wait to be served, and in some places you go up to the counter to order. On one occasion recently, I took my daughter to get a sandwich, and at least three different people were involved in making the sandwich, and when they asked if she wanted certain ingredients, we got really confused because we thought that these other people were making other sandwiches, and wondered why they were asking us. By the time we figured out what was going on, she had a sandwich she didn't like, and we felt totally confused and disorientated. It might be useful if eating establishments displayed their rules so that you knew what to do, and it would make it less stressful. For instance, advice about how to pay, and whether or not you should leave a tip. I have also noticed that people seem to sit around for ages after they have eaten. I can't understand why they would want to do so. I often find it such a stressful experience that I either lose my appetite, or I spill something and I feel like I am drawing attention to myself, and then I get an overwhelming urge to get out of there.

I used to put myself through all sorts of stressful situations, believing that I was doing the right thing. I would take my daughter to toddler group, and sit out of the way next to the stage, hoping that no one would talk to me, because I felt so awkward. I'd watch my daughter, who also has AS, as she sat on her own, and when she did try to interact with other children, usually knocked them over because of her poor co-ordination; and pretty soon we were both given a wide berth by the other mums and children. This continued as my daughter grew up – school concerts and village events. I wanted my daughter to feel like she was a part of the community we were living in, even if her parents weren't. Then all of a sudden, I started questioning why I was doing it. My daughter didn't enjoy it, and I certainly didn't. It was more of an obligation, and I came to the conclusion that I wasn't doing anything wrong by not attending these events. I might be considered unsociable, but I was hardly likely to be missed. I was, however, very anxious about the fact that my daughter seemed to have difficulties in forming friendships, and complained of other children picking on her and being lonely at school.

I was, and still am, an only child, whom my parents described as being very shy. I would talk to people I knew, but there was one neighbour in particular that made me feel very anxious. I think it was because he used to ask me questions when I was going out with my mum, and every time I was unable to hear what he was asking me. I used to think I might be deaf, and I'd ask him to repeat it several times, and I didn't know what to say. However, once we had got away from the situation, I would realize what he'd said. This still happens to me now, particularly if I am feeling nervous. I attended the local primary school, but when I was 11 my parents sent me to a private school because they thought I was too quiet to cope with the local comprehensive. When I had a friend, I tended to have one friend at a time. It was always the other person or circumstances that brought our friendship to an end. I can remember standing in the playground close to the wall, watching all the other children playing or walking round with their friends. I didn't hang around the teachers or dinner ladies, and no one was unkind to me, I just didn't have a friend. On one occasion I became friends with a boy in my class, which was considered to be odd – boys and girls shouldn't be friends at school for some reason. We were only friends during school, and I was really happy when he lent me his Paddington pencil top to take home for the summer holidays. I was also mortified when I lost it, and worried for weeks that he would no longer be my friend.

As it turned out, he still was, but he then emigrated to Australia shortly afterwards. Another girl I made friends with was extremely bossy and spoilt, and I think she liked me because she could boss me about, and I went round with her so that I wasn't on my own. Then she teamed up with someone else, and I can't say that I was too disappointed. I think I definitely came to regard myself as inferior or that there was something wrong with me as time went by. I couldn't understand why my friend would make friends with someone else and stop wanting to be with me, when as far as I knew, I'd never been unkind or nasty to them in any way. This has lead to me feeling very insecure, even as an adult. I remember my first day at secondary school, where someone else I knew was starting at the same time, and she told me she would sit next to me. However, when we got there, she recognized someone else she knew and sat with her instead. The girl that was asked to sit next to me was cross about it, because she wanted to sit next to her friend, and she moved at the soonest opportunity. I think some of the experiences I have had have given me a very negative opinion of myself. I know I have very low self-esteem. Sometimes it's hard for me to find anything about myself that I think other people might like. I have never wanted to be the life and soul of the party type of person or to be incredibly popular, but I have sometimes wondered what it is about certain people that makes everyone want to be their friend or run round after them. I don't suppose I'll ever figure it out. I was never jealous of people as such, but just wondered what is was about them, or maybe about me that made people treat us so differently. When I worked in archaeology, my friend came to visit, and the people I had made friends with started to ignore me and seemed more interested in her. They made her friendship bands, but they didn't make me one. They weren't nasty to me in any way, they just seemed to prefer her company. To be truthful, I probably did feel a bit jealous; but mostly I felt upset and puzzled about why they gave her so much attention, and what it was about her that they liked so much. Or more to the point, what it was about me that they didn't like, and it made me feel that I must be a horrible person in some way. I don't believe now that they disliked me; it was just that there was something about her that they liked better.

Throughout my childhood I did have one particular friend, older than myself, and we saw a lot of each other outside school. Most of the time we acted out our favourite television programmes with cuddly toys, or played schools or hairdressers. As we grew older we re-enacted scenes from our favourite television programme, *Starsky and Hutch*. In fact we acted out the whole of our lives when we were together as if we were those characters. We even made identikits, and kept files on our neighbours about their imaginary crimes, which we eventually convinced ourselves were real. Fortunately for me, this friend moved to my school and I spent my break times with her and her friends.

I tended to be invited to quite a few birthday parties when I was little, and I always felt very nervous. I think it had something to do with going to a strange house. Then there were noisy over-excited children, and you were forced to play games even if you didn't want to. Tea-time was awful, because most of the other children were so loud and greedy and spoke with their mouths full. It's only recently occurred to me that that's maybe why I have always disliked certain foods, because I associate them with birthday parties. I think I quite enjoyed some of my own parties, but I can remember that I always ended up feeling upset and crying afterwards.

When I was younger, I used to go and stay with my cousin who lived by the sea. It has only recently occurred to me just how much his friends used to take advantage of me. I never thought anything of it at the time, because I was only nine or ten, and I wasn't used to playing with groups of children. They were all boys, and I used to be chosen to be goalie – which I thought was quite an honour at the time. I used to be sent to fetch the balls that had gone into other people's gardens. Then there was a game that I would describe as Houdini hide and seek. According to the gang, they had all done it before – and I was tied to the washing line pole with my eyes closed. After I had counted to 100 I had to 'escape' and then find everyone. I didn't manage to escape, but one of the boys' sisters untied me eventually; I didn't manage to find them either. I think they gave up on hiding because I took so long. I don't think they had ever really tried it themselves. The worst thing I can remember was when they told me to chant the name of my cousin's neighbour as she walked past – and again they had supposedly all done it before. It really upset the old lady, and she told my aunt and uncle, and I had to go round to her house and apologize. I felt awful, and I couldn't talk to her again after that, or look her in the eye, or go round to see her any more. I really felt ashamed of myself, and bad because I hadn't thought how she might feel. I don't blame my cousin at all because he is a bit younger than me, and it was really one older boy who was the ring leader as it were, but I felt more angry with myself that I had upset someone else and hadn't considered their feelings.

I wouldn't consider myself to have been bullied at school, rather excluded or ignored by most of the other pupils. One thing I can remember, which I have never liked, is people whispering. Sometimes I would think people were talking about me, or it made me feel very isolated. In my first year at secondary school, my so-called friend used to do this; or she would hide my ruler or rubber and deny she had seen them, then later on wave them in the air and not give them back to me. If I said anything to her about it she used to scratch me with her nails. I remember feeling very isolated during my teenage years, and I put it down to the fact that my parents sent me to a private school, and it was difficult to meet up with other pupils outside school hours, but I now know that this wasn't the case. I used to love listening to music, and still do, and so the people on the posters in my room became my friends during the evenings and at the weekend. I used to talk to them about how I was feeling, but when they answered back they usually only said negative things about me.

I did have a few good friends as I was growing up; I guess I just seem to remember the bad experiences and memories more easily. These friendships never seemed to last too long though. I've never been particularly bothered about having lots of friends, and quite a lot of the time I am aware that I have only been friends with some people because it was better than being on my own, but I think that it was likely to have been a mutual arrangement as such. Or I was tolerated by certain groups of people, like when I started university, well, for a short time at least. During my teenage years and whilst I was at university, I often felt depressed, and this was in part caused by my inability to form and maintain friendships, which sometimes resulted in me harming myself.

During my second year at university I lived in lodgings, as I didn't have a group of friends to share a house or flat with. I became friendly with a girl in the year above me, who told me that I could come round to her house whenever I liked. So, taking her at her word, I spent most of my free time there. She seemed fine with this, but one time there was a house meeting, and the other students she shared with decided that I came round too much, and asked her to tell me not to visit so often. I felt really upset when she told me, and I couldn't understand why they hadn't said something sooner, or why she had made the invitation in the first place. I also felt very bad that I had upset her housemates, and I didn't feel like I was welcome to go round any more.

Throughout my adult life, I have often wondered how friendships work. I think it is very important that you trust the person, and you may share common interests and find them to be likeable. I think you need to be able to accept the person for who they are, so long as they don't do anything that is bad that hurts someone else. I find it very difficult to tell whether someone is my friend, because you know how you feel about a person, but you don't know how they feel about you. So you might consider them to be your friend, but you don't know if they think of you as being their friend.

I have never felt the slightest regret about not keeping in touch with the people I was at school or university with, or people I met in past employment. The majority of people I knew as my daughter was growing up, and whom my partner and I associated with, and even members of my own family, mean nothing to me. When I say they mean nothing to me, I don't mean I don't care about them at all. I wouldn't want anything bad to happen to them, but if I never hear any more about them, then it wouldn't upset me in any way. I don't ever find myself wondering what they might be doing, or enquiring after their well-being. Occasionally, I might meet up with family or people I used to know, and if I get on well with them, for a fleeting instant I might think that it would be nice to stay in touch, but the feeling soon goes again. I guess there are some people with whom I have some kind of relationship, but I'm not sure whether they would be described as friends or not. They tend to be people that I have contact with because of a particular activity, or they may be people I work with, so I only really have any contact with them because they are related to a particular situation. I can still get on very well with some of these people, and am quite happy interacting with them whilst I am there. However, once I have left the place of employment, or no longer take part in the activity, then I have no reason to keep in touch with these people, and am not interested in maintaining contact with them in any way. It's good while you are there to have someone to talk to, or have a laugh with occasionally, but then you will probably meet different people in another situation, and really, all that you had in common was the fact that you were both in the same situation at the same time, sharing a similar experience, and then it's over. I don't want to go out to lunch with my work colleagues, or see these people other than when we need to be together.

I think one of the difficulties that I have, is that I seem to form quite strong attachments to some people. There are a few people that I have met throughout my life that I would call friends. These are the people that I want to keep in touch with and reveal more of myself to, rather than interacting on a superficial level. These are the people I become so absorbed in, probably to the detriment of other things. How I choose to look at it is, so long as I feel it's worthwhile and it is making me more happy than sad, then it's OK. Anyway, getting back to the people whom I do regard as friends, I haven't been able to tell them how I feel. I guess it's partly because I've only really just sussed out myself how I seem to work, and although I wasn't quite sure what was going on, I always had a feeling that it wasn't right in some way, or that the person I was friends with would find it odd or too intense. That's one of the reasons I haven't stayed friends with them I guess.

Another problem is I've never been sure how the other person regards me. I don't know whether they consider me to be their friend, or what kind of friend, or how much they like me and what they think is an appropriate amount of time to be in contact with them. I never dared to ask anyone this. I don't know if I thought that everyone felt like this, but I guess not, because being friends seems to be effortless to most people, and I never did ask any of them or tell them how I felt. This is an area that seems to cause me a lot of anguish, because once I have formed this sort of attachment, I think I can maybe become a bit obsessive, or at least not really know how to deal with it. Quite often I feel like I miss the person a lot, and it makes me feel very sad. As I've grown older, I seem to have recognized that just because you can't be with someone all the time, or keep in touch on a daily basis etc., it doesn't mean that they aren't still your friend. This doesn't actually make me feel any better, and so even though I have worked this out and accepted that this is the way it has to be, it doesn't make it any easier. I find it quite embarrassing to admit that I am like this, but I also realize that you really can't help feeling the way you do. Whether you are happy about having those kind of feelings is another matter, but you still can't stop them from happening. I suppose what you can try and control is how you deal with them, and what course of action you take. So even though I really like a person and enjoy the contact I have with them, it is still a sad experience in some ways.

Sometimes friendships seem to come to a natural end, for instance if a person moves away. I do feel guilty about some of the people I have lost touch with, because it is nothing they have done; but I think I find it easier to cope with feeling guilty, than with some of the other feelings I have related to friendships. For instance, when my friend changed courses and moved to another university, I used to go to see him sometimes, but I never knew when I would next see him, and this uncertainty made me feel quite stressed and upset, and I suppose it reached a point where I couldn't deal with it any more. I miss some people terribly, and then I can't keep the friendship going, because it upsets me too much, and even though I really like the person, I just can't do it any more because it is too difficult. I find it hard to describe what it feels like, but the closest way I can think of describing it, is to imagine what it feels like when you are in a relationship with someone, and it is at the stage where you feel totally in love with and absorbed in that person, and then they have to go away, and imagine how bad it would make you feel and how much you would miss them. I know it's not quite the same, i.e. there is not the same level of intimacy as in a personal relationship, but I think the intensity of feeling is similar, in terms of missing the person, and I have experienced having to leave my partner for a period of time not through my own choice, and so I think this is a fair comparison, at least in my case. I don't know whether it is just me that feels this way, or whether lots of people with autism experience the same sorts of feelings.

I guess, ideally, I need to be able to ask the person whether they are my friend, if they like me, and to have some idea about what they think of me. In an ideal world, it would be useful to be able to ask the person how often they would like to keep in touch, and how often they think it is reasonable to see one another. From my perspective, other people seem to have several friends, and they don't seem to worry about whether the person is their friend, they appear to know instinctively, and they seem to know when or how often they should meet up or contact one another. They seem to be able to take it as it comes. Maybe it has something to do with being friends with more than one person; but I know I can only be real friends with someone in an intense and concentrated way, so there's no way I can be friends with more than one or two people. I'm not really sure how it is for other people, but it seems that they have friends, and are quite secure in the knowledge that the friendship will continue, even if they don't contact the other person for some time or think about them. They seem to be able to switch off and concentrate on other aspects of their lives, like their relationship with their partner, or work, or sporting activities, their family and how they spend their free time. To me a friendship is always on my mind. Sometimes it preoccupies me to the point that I can't concentrate on anything else; and sometimes I am able to push it to the back of my mind for a short while. It's like having a television set switched on inside your mind, and you can turn the volume down, but not totally off, so that it is always there in the background; a distraction, not allowing you to focus fully on anything else.

I suppose there are other issues too, some of which I haven't fathomed out yet. For instance, I tend to be fine with a friend's partner or family, but I don't feel comfortable if they have other friends there. I think it has something to do with my feelings of insecurity, and the fact that I find it difficult to relate to more than one person, or more than one related group of people at a time.

To be honest, not having many friends doesn't bother me in the least. At one time I may have wanted to have more friends, and even though I found socializing difficult, I liked the idea of trying to be sociable. I thought that one day, everything would click and I'd be able to do it. I guess that's probably quite common when you're a teenager. It's quite strange I guess, because on the one hand, trying to fit in with everyone else and trying to make conversation and be friendly is crippling, but on the other hand you think that it is what you want, because it seems to be expected of you, or you think that it might make you happy, when all it does is cause you more anxiety. In the past, my dislike of being sociable has sometimes caused friction in my relationship with my partner, because I do not like having visitors. I see my home as being somewhere I should be able to feel safe and secure, away from the stress and anxiety that other people cause me. I used to react quite badly if my partner invited anyone round without giving me time to get used to the idea, or if someone turned up unexpectedly.

It was quite a relief when I discovered that I had AS about a year ago, that there is a reason why I feel this way, and to be able to think to myself that it doesn't matter how many people I am friends with, so long as I feel happy with it and I can deal with it. I don't feel pressurized any more to have friends. I'm quite happy with having my best friend, who is also my partner, my family and the one good friend I do have. I don't feel like I need any more than that, and it's what I can cope with at the moment.

Chapter 7: The Social World and Me

Kamlesh Pandya

Introduction by Luke Beardon
We are told in no uncertain terms that people with AS have problems with Theory of Mind. The more I get to know different individuals on the spectrum, however, the less convinced I am of this 'fact'. In this chapter Kam describes his clear empathy with individual service users while working as support in a residential service for people with autism. Many other people I know, who also happen to have AS, demonstrate a clear empathic understanding of other people. I find myself questioning, do people with AS lack a Theory of Mind in a general sense, or is it more accurate to suggest that they lack a Theory of Mind with NTs? Could it be argued that within the population of AS, Theory of Mind is not a problem at all? Similarly, can we then say NTs are impaired in their Theory of Mind because they find it so difficult to see things from the perspective of those with AS? It seems to me fairly logical to suggest that neurological differences are surely going to contribute to difficulties in understanding between differing populations; however, within the same neurological population it just may be the case that genuine empathy and understanding is found to be prevalent and common.

Introduction
My name is Kamlesh Pandya but known by my friends as Kam. I am 28 years old and was born in Leicester. I am a British Indian man. I currently

work part time for an organization called Accredo as an outreach support worker with adults who have autistic spectrum disorders (ASD) and Down Syndrome. I have been doing this type of work for nearly four years. Previously I worked for the National Autistic Society (NAS) doing similar work. When I first started, work colleagues and management believed that I was a great investment to the company. They felt I worked very well. I believe I have a very strong understanding of service users and their needs. About two years ago I realized why this might be, because I was diagnosed with Asperger Syndrome (AS), which is a mild form of autism. *[Editors' note: many individuals are informed that AS is a mild form of autism. We do not agree with this description in any way; AS is complex, and the ways in which it can affect an individual may be extreme and not at all 'mild'.]*

Background

In 2002, I remember my younger sister Raksha said to me that I had been very good at looking after Granddad. I used to take him for a walks near our house, trim his toenails, take him to the doctor's, collect his medication, wash, bath and shave him and generally just spend quality time with him. We got on very well, he was like my best friend. We spoke about lots of things together, like how to be a 'good person', he used to tell me stories from the Hindu scriptures, or explain to me what is morally right and wrong and generally anything that a granddad and grandson would do together we did. He even gave me Polo mints and 50p a month! We interacted very well with each other. I knew due to his old age and his visual impairment that he needed lots of support. I met the role as a family carer. It has now been 14 years since Granddad died.

Leading up to a diagnosis

I love rollercoasters and about five years ago I went to Alton Towers with Raksha and her best friend. They both did the kind of work I do currently. We were having a great day, one part I remember really well was the bit that I know now, has changed my life. We were queuing for the Black Hole, I was daydreaming. I always used to get told I live in my own world daydreaming all the time. Whilst queuing, my sister and her best friend were having a conversation on autism, ASD and AS. Normally when people are talking, I do not get involved unless there is something to do with me, or if it is a topic, which I have good understanding of. They mentioned very briefly that whilst working with adults with AS they noticed that I too had some similar behaviours, borderline to people with AS. At first, I did not think too much about it. My knowledge of autism was limited as at the time I was not working for the NAS. When I was at school, teachers, peers at school, even the caretakers thought I was a bit odd and often mischievous but that was as far as it went; the fact that my sister and her friend actually thought my behaviours were similar to that of the people they worked with was a bit strange...

About a year after the above story, my sister mentioned that I would make a good care worker and, if I was interested, I could work with adults with autism. Previously I had not had very rewarding jobs; I have worked in factories, outdoor markets, supermarket and leisure centres and I thought this care worker's role would be the perfect opportunity for me to work alongside others who would appreciate me and my natural ability. When she mentioned it, I thought that I did not stand a chance, I mean OK I know that I had skills taking care of Granddad and I learnt it myself, but sometimes I did doubt whether I was good enough. I also knew that at the time I was 23 years old and thought if I could utilize my skills on each individual person in care as if they were my granddad, it would work. I know it sounds silly but that's the way I think. I decided to go ahead with it.

My sister trained me very well and explained to me what autism was. I have to admit at the time it all seemed like rocket science to me! She explained to me about social interaction, imagination and communication (the triad of impairments). Raksha made it very clear that if I was to be successful I was to try to understand and listen very carefully. She always knew that if I was shortlisted for an interview, I would have a great chance of getting the job. She said it was mostly all about giving employers the right impression, memorizing information concerning the role and making eye contact, even though I find it very difficult to give eye contact. I needed to be clear on what I said so that the opposition would have a good understanding of me – answering questions properly. Thankfully, Raksha worked very hard with me for the interview preparation work. I remember her saying 'I want you to understand last this is a good opportunity and you could get the job if you do your homework' (what she meant by that was if I prepared myself, I would be OK). My impression was because she was serious I had to be because sometimes when people are talking to me they often get the wrong impression that I am not listening to what they are saying. The truth is that I do but I lose track of what people say if their sentences are too long. Therefore, I had to try twice as hard and pay attention to what Raksha said. At the same time, my mum would often say, 'Listen to what she is saying so you do not have to struggle in life'. Another good idea that my sister suggested was that I make some photocopies of the application form because I normally make a lot of mistakes, losing concentration and misspelling words. Sometimes I spell them how they sound, e.g. pneumonia spelt with an 'n' instead of a 'p'. Another mistake I often make is using the wrong words to express myself, I sometimes guess and think something is the right word but it is not. Despite all of this, eventually the form was filled in black ink, it was as neat as and as good as it could be.

A week or so later, a letter arrived through the post and I was offered an interview. My sister went through a process of training me on what they were likely to ask at interview. We did role plays at home for two nights before the interview, which was very helpful.

Before the interview, I got very smartly dressed, I was wearing black trousers, plain white shirt, tie and black blazer; I had my record of achievement folder with up-to-date qualifications and black shoes polished to a shine. I remember Dad saying, 'When you go for a job interview it's so important that you dress smart,' and he showed me how to knot a tie like they do on the TV. It was all about making the right first impression.

At the interview, I made very strong eye contact: I looked very clearly at both interviewers and answered their questions from how we practised at home. I remembered word for word what my sister said. It was almost as if I was answering to my sister and I used this technique to my advantage, as a result it made me feel very confident in the room. I was finding it hard to make eye contact but I knew if I wanted the job and to earn money I needed to step away from my 'comfort zone' (as my sister would call it) or it was scrubbing toilets and mopping floors! Deep down I knew I could not afford to make any mistakes of any form.

After two weeks, they offered me the job and I was so happy: thrilled, full of joy. If you have ever seen a film called *The Shawshank Redemption*, it felt like escapism, a bit like when Tim Robbins escapes Shawshank prison for his freedom, it is a great film. That is how I felt, I mean mopping floors and scrubbing toilets in factories was not using my true skills.

At first, I had some shadowing shifts at an autism organisation and I found it very difficult to make friends, all kinds of thoughts were going through my mind. Because when you work for an organization, you want to make a good impression so that work colleagues can offer you friendship and help you feel comfortable. Nevertheless, sometimes I think that I do not have the confidence because I often felt unsure as to why they were not talking to me. Why they were looking at me in a horrible way, I could not understand why I was being ignored or why they were laughing at me on some days. Even though it may not have been personal, I did find it hard to understand people's body language and facial expressions. Socializing with neurotypical (NT) people is not my biggest strength; I find it hard.

It was a real big struggle the first year of working at an autsim organisation. I focused on working hard with service users who had autism, so that they could get to know me and I could get to know them. A lot of them did not speak or, if they did speak, they would only say a few words. I wanted to interact with them, they often jumped up and down, laughing loud, giggling, holding my hand, crying. At the time, I did not feel comfortable with the staff as they were not nice to be around. Many of the things that the staff were talking about did not really interest me in any sort of way. I felt that even if I wanted to be friends with them I could not, as I did not share their hobbies or interests. It was obvious that I was very isolated and I felt very much alienated. Even though I was friendly, polite and kind it made very little difference to them, although I remember that there was a couple of staff members that were nice to me.

When it came to service users, I could really understand them. I connected very well with them, it was the kind of thing I used to do when I was younger:

- challenging behaviour
- getting anxious and cross when there was a change
- needing a lot of reassurance and support
- being impatient waiting around
- having mood swings from high to low
- having your own personal space, spending time on your own
- repetitive behaviours
- copying others
- constant thoughts and emotions
- talking to myself out loud

- some days feeling high full of energy, excitement, very happy full of excitement and joy, other days feeling tired and worn out
- problems with sleep patterns
- struggling to relate to others.

I can honestly say the examples above are things I go through in everyday life. To this day, when working with different service users I strongly now notice similarities between them and me. It was like meeting people whom you just get on with, there were no judgements, stereotypes or discrimination between us. Most of the time when you work with service users, all they really want is for you to spend as much time with them as possible. We rolled a ball, sat down having tea and lunch, blowing at each other's faces, copying each other, smiling, laughing watching TV and listening to music, just spending quality time.

Two years went by, I kept myself to myself, distant from other staff. When other staff worked with the same service users, a lot of them were physically targeted and could not work with certain service users. Female staff often had their hair pulled, faeces thrown at them, or they got bitten; whereas with me, it was the opposite, I rarely got targeted in the three years.

Staff and management noticed strong similarities in behaviours between myself and some of the service users. There was a suspicion that I might have AS. Staff gossiped about me being 'weird', especially the female staff, saying how I was 'connecting' with clients who had autism and doing things that they were doing or copying their behaviours. The truth is sometimes AS is not recognized until very late on in life. Some people may never ever get a diagnosis because it is a hidden disability. Maybe working at an autism organisation was a good thing for me as it strengthened the suspicion of my AS.

I started to wonder why both my family and people at work might have been saying that I had AS tendencies. It made me think there must be some truth here. In the past, people have always made horrible comments that I am weird and abnormal. Like for example I have always had full on conversations with myself in the bedroom, bathroom or whenever I need reassurance about something that might have happened in the day. Or for example I go for long walks at two in the morning, sometimes I am rude to people and I do things the same way over and over again. Sometimes I do not want to speak to anyone, because I have so many thoughts in my mind and I just need to be on my own. I sometimes lock myself in my room for personal space. When I am in my room I get all kinds of thoughts going through my head and it can often make me feel isolated from people.

Diagnosis

All of these behaviours eventually led to a diagnosis. I trusted my sister, she mentioned to me about the possibility of me having some type of ASD. She asked me to think about and then decide if I wanted to go and see a doctor. I thought about it and decided to go ahead with it.

My sister and I went to see our local general practitioner (GP). It was the most uncomfortable moment I had to go through, I did not have the confidence in talking to the GP. To our frustration, the doctor did not know what autism was. He said he did not know what to do. Luckily, my sister and I knew of the professor's name at the local mental health unit.

A month later, I received an A4 brown envelope in the post, which contained questionnaires for my parents to complete on my childhood to adulthood growing-up process. Once that was sent off, two weeks later, I was offered an appointment by the professor to go and see him with my mum, dad and sister. I was feeling nervous and was not sure what to expect. The professor was nice and asked me some questions. I answered them to the best of my ability. One question that the professor asked me was, could you give me some examples of problems you have faced in life. I told him that I find it hard to understand when people are joking or if they are being serious. I gave him two good examples. The first was when I was working out in the gym some pretty-looking woman came up to me and said, 'Are you seeing anyone?' My immediate reaction was, is she referring to me as if I'm blind? I answered by saying, 'I'm not visually impaired, I see people all the time, it is natural for human beings to see people.' Then I started going into to detail like I normally do such as talking about the iris, pupil, conjunctiva and optic nerves. She got very offended and at that point, she walked off. I automatically thought, well, that is very rude of her and I never saw her again. One of gym instructors came up to me and said, 'What did you do and why did she walk off?' I said 'Well, she asked me if I was seeing anyone and I told her I see people all the time.' I explained all of this to the gym instructor in great detail. By this point the gym instructor started to laugh and I could see tears were coming out of his eyes. I still could not work out what was so funny. He said 'You are absolutely unbelievable! A tall attractive woman with blonde hair wanted to ask you out and you said "I see people all the time!"' Later on when it was quiet in the gym he explained and said, 'What she really might have meant was perhaps or maybe she would have liked a boyfriend type of relationship with you.' I thought to myself, 'Well why didn't she say that in the first place?' and I remember him telling me that she would expect you to know that because people don't always use literal words and say things as how you expect them to be.

The other example I gave to the professor was when a woman at work said to me, 'I lost two pounds last week'. I said to her, 'Where did you leave it last? Was it in your purse before you lost it?' I remember her looking at me as if she was shocked or stunned. Then she explained, 'No what I mean was I lost two pounds in weight.' The first thing that came in my mind was a two-pound gold coin, which has Queen Elizabeth's image on it. If you think about it, this is United Kingdom, we use pounds, how did weight come across as pounds? I really could not work it out.

After one hour he asked me, 'Do you know what AS is?' I told him I have worked with clients who have ASD but I know very little about AS, as I normally work with clients who have autism.

Accepting the diagnosis of AS

The process of diagnosis is very stressful and painful to accept, especially when you have had a mainstream life throughout your existence. Suddenly when you get the diagnosis you have to learn to accept a new identity, except it is technically something that you already are but have not known of.

It has taken me two years to fully accept what I am and who I am and in that time, there were support groups available. I was glad that my family fully supported me. It was agreed that I was not going to attend any of the support groups because the people who I would meet would be people who are service users, whereas I don't fit in with them because I'm very high functioning – the fact that I can hold a job, hold a relationship, do things and manage myself.

As much as I wanted to have friends who have AS, the problem I was facing was that I have not met anyone who is like me in Leicester. Therefore, I decided to do my own research and find other AS people who were more like me. By doing so, I found a website called Aspies for Freedom. My concern was that Aspies for Freedom was an international Asperger site, it was not UK based and it did not provide me with the local knowledge and social side that I needed.

Eventually, I found a website called Aspie Village (see Chapter 8 for a more in-depth discussion of this) and it was a site for people with AS who are predominantly UK citizens which people from England, Northern Ireland, Scotland and Wales could use. I introduced myself to other people with AS; as a newly diagnosed man the most positive thing about Aspie Village was that there were so many of us with AS. We are all very different in our social and communication skills. I wanted to meet AS people like me, which I could not find in Leicester. I class myself as very interactive and talkative as a person, not shy. I will speak my mind and ask questions until I understand the information. It took me one year to find the right people, people who were like me. I now go on day trips. Just by talking to them online, we arrange to go to cafés, quiet bars and museums. I enjoy going on the trips. I feel like my online friends have helped me to come to terms with the diagnosis. I was amazed to know that there are people like me who have gone through the same difficulties that I did when I was younger. It is hard for others to see because AS is a hidden disability, classed as a neurological disorder. This affects a lot of males and females. We are different to neurotypical people (NTs) we think and interpret the world differently to NTs. My examples are shown in the diagram.

In the diagram I am demonstrating how my life is, people who I have made friends with online also experience the similar things in life to me.

Culture and family

This is probably the hardest thing I am writing in this chapter so here goes! When it comes to extended family/guests I find it boring to interact with them when they come round to visit my mum and dad. In my culture I am expected as the man in the house to be welcoming, sincere and have an etiquette. It is almost an unsaid rule. I know I am Hindu but when they talk about things that don't really interest me I really struggle to conform. I cannot relate to anything that they talk about. Other times I just start daydreaming and not listening to what they say. Sometimes I create funny pictures of them in my head with them having elephant trunks coming out of their faces. Once an overweight lady who was wearing a sari (our national dress worn traditionally by Indian woman) came to visit my mum: she reminded me of a bouncy ball. Generally, I just struggle to offer

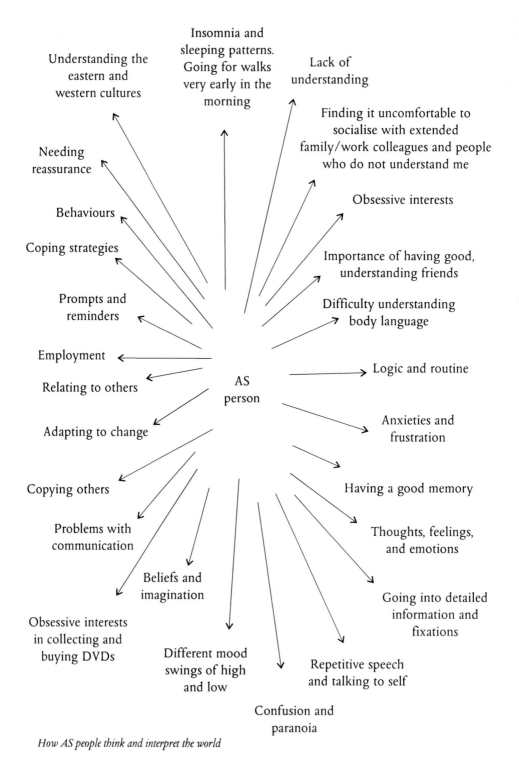

How AS people think and interpret the world

anything towards the conversations that the guests are having with my family. Sometimes if they are talking about science, I can become interested in the subject.

My mother endlessly goes on about me not spending time with the family and she often thinks I can be seen as rude towards the family. In my world, the way I see it is, I am someone who loves snooker, computers, museums, play station and the gym and if they do not want to talk about those things, I will not be interested in them.

Relationships

Being in a relationship can be scary as you are expected to call girlfriends, be understanding even if you don't feel like it and generally be nice. When I was in a relationship for the first time, I did not have my AS diagnosis. Despite my AS tendencies my girlfriend at the time called my behaviours 'special'. I liked that. I hadn't been called that nice word before. We lasted for four and a half years. In my second relationship I struggled a bit as I often compared the two women in my head. The first one had called me more and she constantly texted me, the second one was more independent and did less of the phoning and texting which made me confused as I thought every woman should be like the first one! So later we split up.

Having relationships with these women, what I have now slowly learnt is that everyone is different and relationships are a learning process. They are not all the same like clones; women are a bit like fingerprints or DNA, all different, never one the same. Being in a relationship is about learning what each other likes and dislikes and through this finding out your compatibility.

Socializing with work colleagues

Normally whenever I am invited to a work do with staff and we go to a bar or restaurant I find that they are all involved in a conversation. Again, this has very little interest to me so, as a coping strategy, I blank everyone out whilst sitting next to them and start to think of insects or animals that most people would not like, such as spiders or scorpions. I store the image in my mind, then find a serviette/tissue and start to build the image from my mind on to the table. Many people find me amusing and others find it socially inappropriate; according to them it's not normal behaviour. For me it is escapism.

Chapter 8: Aspie Village: A Web-Based Social Forum

Dean Worton

Introduction by Luke Beardon

The idea of Aspie Village is a sublime one. The way in which Dean describes it exudes Asperger friendliness, welcoming and support. With technology still moving forward at a good pace (and who knows how many individuals with AS we have to thank for that) in time the idea might be extended to virtual reality environments complete with visuals. I think that this could be one of the most supportive ways for individuals with AS to develop and practise their skills in a safe, non-sensory, non-threatening environment which may then enable them to widen their experiences in the 'real' world. The other aspect of the Village that is so exceptional is the care, dedication and thought that Dean and other moderators have put in, in terms of making the site as welcoming as possible to new members and making sure as many individual needs are taken into account as possible. Once again, I believe this demonstrates a well-developed 'Aspie Theory of Mind'. If I had AS I certainly think the Village would be my first port of call.

The teens

Throughout my school life, although I always had a friendship group, close friendships always fizzled out. In the first half of my teens, while my peers were out enjoying themselves, I stayed in. It was only in my late teens that I started to have any real sort of social life. I became part of a friendship group, but this involved all the hallmarks of the NT social world, spending every evening and weekend in each other's company, going to pubs every night and doing other things that I didn't really want to do. I had some good times but also suffered from a great deal of anxiety as I felt that I was not able to be myself or even to be by myself. Only one friendship from that time remains but this friend after spending time with me was able to see a positive side of me that my AS had masked when in group situations.

University

When I went away to university, I was finally able to be by myself. The problem was, however, that far from being in friendship groups that I was uncomfortable with, it seemed to be more the other way round. I made friends at the start of the course, and we seemed to get on well, but after a few months my company appeared to be unwanted despite my efforts. I ended up feeling a bit lonely. It might not have bothered me much if I had been living with my parents, but I was sharing accommodation with people who had their own lives to lead, and it was a 'treat' if they ever invited me to the pub. In my second year, my social contact at university was almost non-existent although I happened to have a part-time job: whilst this didn't produce any actual friendships, the contact I had with my colleagues at work did help to some extent to make up for this and in some ways it didn't matter because I only had to be in classes for 14 hours a week. In the third year, I spent a study year abroad. I had no friends in my class but outside my class got on very well with a number of French, British and Irish people, especially in the halls of residence and had the best time of my life with them. Some of these were at my university the next year, which did slightly improve my social contact in my final year. Sadly, I'm no longer in touch with any of the friends I made over there. Friendships come and go. After leaving university, I bumped into a school friend and we became friends again, although we don't meet very often due to our own unique circumstances.

Entering the Asperger social world

In January 2000, which is quite apt as it is the first month of the millennium (even though it's technically 2001), following some problems I'd been experiencing, my mother introduced me to AS. Eventually, a relative introduced me to the local AS support group. I was disappointed to find no other AS adults there (or no others wanting to admit to it) so I told the organizer that I wanted to meet adults with AS. He gave me some website addresses. I joined a penpal website and got writing to other Aspies.

Writing to others with Asperger Syndrome from all over the world and chatting live with them through instant messaging was a great experience. We had had so many of the same experiences and we felt instantly accepted by each other. An Aspie living in New York city opened up a message board and chat room which I joined. Through this I met a very wide range of Aspies from all over the world. I was approached by a member in the United Kingdom who wanted to set up something similar just for Aspies in the UK, the greatest difference being that it would host real-life meet-ups where people with Asperger Syndrome would all meet in real life and find out what others with Asperger Syndrome were really like and you could make real-life friendships with them.

My own website

Eventually, I had my own ideas and set up my own site. I built it around the theme of a village as I wanted it to feel like a village full of people with Asperger Syndrome, because I thought, what better way to make socially isolated people feel part of something?

Some Aspie websites attract a lot of seemingly socially able people whose interactions are not far removed from the NT majority, which is something that many Aspies want to get away from. My website operates in a different way to others, and while we get the inevitable grumbles from those who want a rowdy place where people are at loggerheads with each other, on the whole it's a well-accepted ethos, because people do feel supported. The main thing about the site is that it doesn't patronize people. Myself and the others who run the site are people who have AS and do struggle with many things in the mainstream world, but are able to draw upon our own collective experiences to know where the other people are coming from. As such we have rarely banned anyone from the site.

The site currently has about 200 members and this is set to grow, yet we have been able to continue with our village-like friendly atmosphere. There are naturally some disagreements between some of the stronger characters, but because of our ethos of having a warm and cosy environment, the members usually keep it down to a dull roar. You'd think with

200 different Aspies with varying degrees of difficult mindsets, there would be utter chaos, yet there is a surprising solidarity about the group and some great friendships have formed.

In the early days, I used to spend a lot of my spare time answering people's pleas for support of some kind and generally encouraging them to see themselves in a positive light and try to give them a bit more confidence in themselves. I'm not sure if any replies I've ever made have improved anyone's life for good, but advice I've given has certainly helped people in some situations. So many people have now joined the group that I no longer need to reply to pleas to support as often, as on any given day, no matter what someone posts on the site, there will usually be a few people ready and waiting to reply to them on the very same day. This brings the members together with even greater ease than ever before and there is a true sense of community, thus living up to the tag of 'Village'.

Inevitably the dynamics of the group could easily change as the member size increases beyond 200 people. In a village with fewer than 200 people, those who take part in the life of the village would know quite a lot of other villagers and it would feel friendly and safe, yet if an extra 100 or 200 people moved into the village, it would of course start to feel more crowded. We have taken action to prevent this needing to be a problem and the way we have done this is to use the analogy of a real-life growing village, though not a specific one. If there is a pub, church, village hall, school, post office and shop, the rest of the village would generally grow up around this. With the growth of the village, these facilities would become slightly busier.

In the case of my website, the busier parts of the village have remained; however, we have created an area where members are able to get away from the hustle and bustle of the rest of the village if they wish to do so. This could be likened to a meadow at the edge of the village. Originally this area was entitled 'Secret Garden'. However, when this forum was mentioned to the main body of the membership, there was some concern from a few regular users that this could create divisions in the group so the name of the quiet area was changed to something more inclusive sounding, and all members of at least one week's standing are welcome to join the quiet area with the simple proviso that they post something into it within three months of subscribing to it and again at yearly intervals. This seems like a reasonable compromise in order to keep it as a forum with a very low readership. This way, it would probably take a while for more than 100 people to be users of the quiet area, and should the member size of my website ever become as big as some of the international sites with hundreds of members, we will simply adapt and gradually add more hidden forums. We have had recent feedback that a few of the people who post regularly don't like the idea of too many forums that require an extra membership and that for some Aspies it could become confusing and stressful to have to make special subscriptions to so many forums if they wish to become members of them. Therefore, we have listened to their views and decided to meet them halfway and only introduce hidden forums at a slow pace. However, as the membership grows, we do feel that there may be an opportunity for having subscription-only forums for specific hobbies and interests.

Fictional scenario

Adam is 37 years old, goes to work from nine to five, doesn't interact much with his colleagues and has no social life. He lives on his own, has no partner and no children and feels very lonely. It's Christmas 2008 and fed up with watching repeats on satellite television, he decides to hook up to the world wide web. He types in search terms on the internet such as 'lonely', 'anxious', 'different from other people', and finds my website. He reads some of the messages and it resonates with him. There are people with similar experiences to Adam and he wonders if he has this thing called Asperger Syndrome, he reads further and diagnoses himself. He joins the site and sees the Member Introductions and Greetings section. He feels that it would only be polite to post an introduction. He gets halfway through and to the side of the screen he notices that there are 627 members. He then imagines 626 other people all being able to read about his problems and feels that this seems a rather daunting prospect, so he doesn't send the message.

He browses the site and is wishing that there was somewhere he could offload his problems without that many people reading. He sees that the site has a chat room and there are only a few people in there chatting, so he goes in there. He says 'Hello' and so do the other people. They are friendly to him, but he finds it hard to follow the pace of the chat and they are cracking lots of jokes. Adam takes things quite literally and doesn't have a well-developed sense of humour. He doesn't feel comfortable in the chat room and leaves, never to go back there.

He then looks at some more messages and stumbles upon a forum about collecting. Adam collects stamps and so he subscribes to the collectors' forum. There are other people posting messages about stamps. In fact, there is one member who has the one rare stamp, which would complete one of his collections and is willing to exchange this for a stamp that Adam has two of. At first, Adam is wary of replying but really wants that stamp. He procrastinates and eventually finds out that there are only 58 people in the collectors' forum. He can cope with this and replies to the message posted by Roger659. Roger is very welcoming to Adam and asks him a bit about himself. Adam reluctantly replies and Peter replies: apparently he has a friend who lives near Adam. Roger, Adam and Peter start sending each other private messages and eventually meet up in London and go to a stamp exhibition and then go out to a pub afterwards. Adam has not been in a pub for five years as he never had anyone to go to one with. He feels comfortable sitting there in the pub with Roger and Peter and after not speaking an awful lot during the rest of the day, he opens up and starts talking about his love of stamps. He becomes best of friends with the two men and they all travel to visit each other. Adam becomes so relaxed around Roger and Peter that in time he can talk to them animatedly about stamps and sometimes even discusses his difficulties with Asperger Syndrome and Roger and Peter also open up about their problems. Adam has been reluctant to mention that he is not actually diagnosed until one day it comes out that Roger has never been for a diagnosis either. Peter gives each of them the name of the professional which diagnosed him who was very good, very cheap and only made him wait one month for the appointment.

Member focus

My website is a very member-focused group and, while it would be impossible to please every individual, we work hard to meet the needs of as many members as possible, and have therefore made a compromise so that while making changes to our original plans in order to reduce feelings of segregation, we have not simply abandoned the idea of the quieter forum as we know that the members who are more likely to want such a forum are less likely to speak out about this fact. Even if only five people exchange posts in that forum, its still worthwhile as those five people are integrating with someone and feeling the benefit of posting, something which would not happen if they were too uncomfortable to post in front of 300 to 400 people.

Role play

Another way that we make the members feel a part of something is that each member who wishes has a role in the village. This doesn't mean that anyone literally has to carry out their role as it's all make-believe. My website is not a real village, it's a fictional village and only comes to life through the posts written in the role play part of the Village Green sub-group. The moderators are the village councillors who take turns at being mayor, one of which is the local landlord and has a tunnel from his shop to his old TV repair shop. We have our own TV station, and transport everywhere you look – including three railway stations, several bus services and even an orbital monorail service. Each shop is run by a member of the website and even the older members join in. The existence of this fictional village doesn't wipe away the problems of those who join the website, but for a few minutes each day members can bring a smile to their faces by taking themselves away into this quirky little village where there are many others like them and, because it involves interacting with real people, can almost make the village itself and their roles in it seem real.

Chat room

Some members aren't big fans of exchanging messages with each other and this is where the chat room facility comes in. Due to the busy lives of myself and the other moderators, its not always possible to organize pre-arranged chats. For that reason, the chat room is available 24 hours a day and the way that a crowd gathers is that, when entering the site, it's possible to see if someone has gone into the chat room. There are enough people logging into the site in any one hour that they are usually spotted and joined by another member or 'villager'. It's rare for more than ten people to be in the chat room at the same time. Its normal for there to be about four or five people at any one time, and this works well. There is even a facility to 'whisper' to an individual member as long as they are in the chat room at the time. Therefore the chat room is a great way to get to know other Aspies away from the site through exchanging email addresses, and anything you may have had to type in the chat room prior to forming this friendship was probably only seen by half a dozen or fewer people. Usually, when someone enters the chat room, even if they have never been in there before, most people say hello to them.

If I encounter a new member in the chat room, I usually try to make them feel welcome, although I don't get 'in their face' by asking them lots of questions. As with interacting with members on the message board or if I meet them in real life, I try to interact enough to draw them into the community without interacting so much that they feel uncomfortable and put on the spot and never come back. Now and again, chat nights are even arranged to celebrate members' birthdays and set up as though those turning up were going to a party together. We make believe that we are in the village pub and possibly drinking Aspie Brew which is a fictional drink. How wonderful to be able to go out for a drink in a pub without leaving your armchair and without a hangover. If someone turns up to the chat who doesn't like the role play, we do, however, try to switch it off as, again, we want everyone to be comfortable and to want to return again and again.

Meet-ups

We hold regular meet-ups and members sometimes arrange small gatherings in their local area. The reason behind the meet-ups was to give adults with Asperger Syndrome the opportunity to meet other people with Asperger Syndrome and to be treated normally. You can just turn up and take as much or as little out of it as you like. You can bring someone else along with you if you wish. We do generally request not to bring more than one other person with you because Aspies sometimes dislike big crowds, but if someone can't attend otherwise then we do make an allowance. It's even OK to bring a child along. The first time someone brought a child along, I did ask the other attendees in advance if it was OK by them, as I like every individual on a meet-up to feel comfortable on the day. I do realize that it can't always be possible to please all of the people all of the time, but by considering people's individual needs minor adjustments can make for a very pleasant day. Everyone was fine about a child being present.

Before every meet-up, I do forward planning with individuals' needs in mind. These are usually very subtle things that the other attendees don't even notice. For example, with very few exceptions we have always met up in a railway station. The start time is usually 12 p.m., and we do ask that people who have difficulty with this make this clear. This way people are never much later than 12 p.m. except when its unavoidable. Much earlier than 12 p.m. and it makes people anxious because they either struggle to arrive that early or are stressed out while we wait for everyone else. I then search the internet to find out if that station has a café or pub where we can meet up. If someone is bringing a child, I will ring the pub to find out if children are allowed. The other good thing about meeting in a pub or café is that if one member of the group doesn't arrive until 12.45 p.m., we can start the meet-up right there. We usually set off almost as soon as the last person arrives. In some cases, someone might not arrive until 1.30 p.m. and we might stay on in the same pub getting to know each other rather than putting that person through the stress of trying to find us somewhere else. This does, however, depend on the particular individuals present. I always ask each person if they are happy to stay in the pub or café a bit longer. If someone is particularly anxious by staying in the pub or café either the others will agree to move on or, if they prefer to stay put, I will find some sort of compromise.

If there doesn't appear to be anywhere other than the waiting room to sit down in the station, I try to plan around the incoming trains. I generally in this case alter the start time to 12.30 p.m. so that we are not waiting around too long if someone is late, as 12.30 p.m. is easier to make than 12 p.m. If someone is going to be very late, I will make special arrangements to meet them when they arrive without it needing to be too annoying to other people present. Occasionally, we might have to wander about that bit more to be able to meet the late arrival, but its all part of the experience and makes the day more interesting. After all we're Aspies, so something would be wrong if everything was 100 per cent perfect all the time. If anything, it breaks the ice. People make allowances for each other, just as they would expect the others present to make allowances for them. It has never reached the point where one person's needs were so great that it impinged on the entire meet-up. However, even if someone had such great personal needs that the only way to have them met would be to work around that person that is what would happen.

Generally speaking, meet-ups tend to be divided into three 90-minute-long activities. This is to allow for the fact that what one Aspie likes another will dislike and it won't always be possible to satisfy each and every person present. It tends to be 90 minutes in a pub and/or café, 90 minutes outdoors (weather permitting) and 90 minutes in a minor tourist attraction. This of course is variable according to the size of the group and personal preferences to those who turn up on the day. It's tailored to satisfy as many people as possible. Everyone has the opportunity to have their say about what they want to do or not do. Naturally, not everyone will be happy with what we end up doing, but 80 per cent of people report enjoying the meet-up and at least 20 out of the 50 or so people who have so far been on a meet-up have attended a subsequent meet-up. Every meet-up has had at least one person on their first meet-up and for the past two years there have been no meet-ups that haven't attracted repeat custom.

An ideal amount of people on a meet-up in my opinion is six people, it's not too many and not too few. The average number is probably closer to eight people, though in less populated areas less than this is more likely. The South East tends to attract slightly more people. Interestingly, the meet-ups with greatest attendance have seemed to run the smoothest of all. Of course the distinct advantage is that you get to meet a greater variety of Aspies and have a better chance of meeting a like-minded Aspie to yourself. Even in the biggest meet-ups, no one is ever completely forgotten about. What I don't do is impose on anyone, but if someone doesn't appear to have really been spoken to much, I always strike up a conversation with them. I do this in a very gentle way by asking questions that they are likely to be happy to answer. For instance, if they have posted something about a hobby on the website, I will ask them about this hobby and this usually breaks the ice. In any case, I think I've spoken to every person who has attended a meet-up. I tend to keep each conversation to about five minutes unless the other person makes it longer. This way, each person present feels acknowledged and respected, yet if they find conversations uncomfortable this is respected by myself, as I operate each and every meet-up in such a way that each member feels comfortable.

No member is ever forced into an uncomfortable situation by a meet-up host. For example, we would never start giving someone a pep talk on eye contact or about anything else for that matter. We get enough of that sort of thing from the neurotypical majority. The point of meet-ups is not to feel judged. Meet-ups take place simply so that adult Aspies can meet others like them and for no other reason. Therefore, we accept people as they are and we simply provide the opportunity for those present to meet others like them without any barriers. As stated above, if an individual needs a special arrangement to be made to allow this to happen, then this will be accommodated and others will tend to accommodate this too through mutual co-operation. At the end of the day, everyone wants to meet other Aspies and can make allowances in order to do this.

Again with the idea around the hidden forums, if the website grows to several hundred people, if the meet-ups start to attract more people than before, we would start to make some of the meet-ups more interest based. For example, instead of 20 people going on a meet-up in London, there would be perhaps one meet-up based around sitting in one or two pubs and another that simply visits one or two museums. Bowling seems to be a popular Aspie activity and many like hiking, so these ideas would probably be floated if meet-ups became really popular since it's unlikely that big numbers would attend themed meet-ups. However, meet-ups in their current format will probably still continue. Even if any future meet-ups ever do reach 20 or more attendees, there will still be meet-ups in smaller groups to fall back on.

It would perhaps be ideal if there were some meet-ups with several people and some with a few, since while some people are at a disadvantage in large groups, others prefer the relative anonymity of them. Furthermore, meet-up hosts do tend to speak to every individual present at a meet-up, but it is not always easy to spend time with every individual if the group is a big one. We also recognize if someone prefers to be an observer and after an initial conversation with them will allow them to do this. Often if I worry that a member may have been neglected on a meet-up, they still return. Not everyone likes to be spoken to all the time, while others do. Like most other meet-up hosts, I recognize when someone wants to chat and when they don't. We accept everyone as they are and treat them as they appear to wish to be treated. Usually everyone present feels respected not only by the hosts but also by each other.

Social strategies
Overall, the advice I would give other Aspies on social relationships is not to measure their success in these in terms of the social relationships they have had or attempted to have with the neurotypical majority. Always bear in mind that some neurotypical people have a pack mentality. By not spending time trying to be the same as everyone else, you are finding enough time to be more of an individual. Some young people probably take a few years to find out who they really are simply because they are

trying to live up to some role model who may well themselves simply be following the crowd. There is a good person inside you and don't let anyone else tell you differently. If you learn to respect yourself, there is more chance that others will respect you too. At the same time, don't set out to impress. If you work on your mental health, you will find it easier to relate to people socially and for them to like you. Think of times when you have done something well, been praised and how good you felt. Then think about something which you are good at and the positive things about you. Think about how you could please people using your positive points at some point in the future, close your eyes and imagine yourself stood a few feet in front of you at a point a few years in the future, make the image as positive as you like. It doesn't matter if you picture yourself as prime minister or the next James Bond. Its not about what you actually will be doing in the future, its about feeling like a worthwhile person who won't allow their social confidence to be zapped by unwritten social rules which are set by the status quo. Dare to be an individual. OK, so you may have to be subtle about how you go about it, as sadly you could be ridiculed if you are too obvious about showing unusual traits. Ultimately, however, if people can't accept you as you are, don't bother with those people. There are people out there who will respect your individuality. If you still struggle to be accepted by everyday people, then indeed look on the internet for a website for people with Asperger Syndrome. It's a great starting point!

Chapter 9: Understanding and Enjoying Successful Social Relationships

Wendy Lawson

Introduction by Luke Beardon

Wendy writes very well on how to develop social relationships, and the need to recognize differences in other people. This is critical in terms of the development of the wider social sector, and yet another area that NTs are not altogether good at. We live in a society that seems to be almost dominated by global 'rules' or 'policies' about what is 'best' for people. The problem with this is that what may be best for the majority of people will almost certainly not be best for the minority. And, all too often, that minority includes people with AS. Thus policies such as 'inclusion' need to be adapted, made specific to individuals rather than a group or population – otherwise the very real danger is that everyone will be 'treated' as a homogenous group rather than as the individual they clearly are. Almost by definition people with AS will be unique individuals with their own, often very different, wishes, needs, learning styles and ambitions. Similarly, individuals with AS may well have their own unique way of having friends, developing relationships and being with other people in social settings. To allow this to happen the NT world should recognize that simply doing things in a way that benefits a majority is not good enough for those with AS.

According to Wikipedia (http://en.wikipedia.org/wiki/Social_relations, accessed 15 January 2008) '"Social" connotes association, co-operation, mutual dependence and belonging.' It also suggests that common agreement of its definition is lacking, that the term is used in social science and that even some university departments use the term to describe their field of study. The second part of this term, 'relationships', implies a connection or a shared 'common' goal. Therefore, one could think of 'social relationships' as an existing or developing connection of a social nature. This might apply to a group of individuals located by gender, family, interest or/and common goal.

For some of us the term 'social' conjures up particular images and feelings that might not be 'comfortable', nor encouraging. Although social relationships will mean different things to different people, for those of us who find the concept scary this chapter might be helpful.

Social relationships are unavoidable and, for some of us, are desirable. But, how can we aim to create good social relationships that are comfortable, workable and rewarding? For some of us a social gathering implies relaxed and inviting; unlike a formal gathering, which implies formality, ritual and rules. In many ways, when relationships are 'formalized' and come with rules and specific roles, it is easier to work out what is required. In this chapter I hope to create a picture that informs the reader of the rules underpinning the social understanding that then assists with social relationships. This chapter will also offer some practical illustrations for developing good social relationships.

Each of us is born and grows up in a society inhabited by other humans. Mostly, these humans will live in family environments and will operate much like a team, working together to get things done. All 'social' relationships, therefore, imply a sharing of time and interaction. For many of us, it's the interaction status that we find difficult!

The other difficulty with social relationships is to do with timing and with motivation. If you are a typical individual you will probably enjoy interacting and relating to a cross-section of people, whether or not they share the same interests as you. Your motivation, apart from shared interest, will be to be thought well of and to be viewed as a 'good' person. Quite often support for the concept of social relationships, is based in ideas that community, sharing, being thought well of and performing to meet the expectations of others, is the norm. However, although it might be 'the norm' amongst neurotypicals, those of us who are on the autism spectrum might not be governed by the same motivators and our 'norm' might be differently based. Therefore, once it is understood that social relating is based upon societal expectation and typical societal norms, I think it might be easier to acquire such skills, if you would like to have them. See *Build Your Own Life* (Lawson 2003) and *Friendships the Aspie Way* (Lawson 2005) for a fuller explanation of these points.

Great social relationships exist in various insect colonies. Ants and bees, for example, demonstrate how, as an entity, they can work well together for the greater good of the colony. In other words, even if we don't feel as if we are a particularly social animal (not into parties, clubbing, dancing or group activities) we can still be concerned with the greater good of those around us and work on creating good social relationships. This means, that although we might not 'feel' like being sociable, because our families or friends might need us to be, we can be. For their sake we choose to relate in the manner they expect or need of us.

'My timing is off'

If our 'timing' of appropriate interaction is difficult to work out, then we might need a bit of help. In other words, the timing of our contributions to conversations, actions and even inactivity can be untimely according to typical expectation, so, gaining some support would be useful. We can access the support we need by giving permission to our friends and family so they feel OK about informing us of the things they need from us. At times this might be their need for us to stop talking, to join in a conversation, to help with chores or to join a game and so on.

It is interesting that it's not only AS individuals who find social relating difficult. Many NT individuals in our schools and colleges find it difficult to 'fit in' socially too. They often want to join in with the other students; they want to belong. However, they may be shy, embarrassed or not be good at making the first move. So, sometimes our personalities can be a factor in how we relate socially.

Another issue is the political and 'social' climate that we are brought up in. Where once segregation, distinct roles, separate fashions and gender dominance were the 'in' thing, now inclusion, one size fits all and 'unisex' are the norm. Along with these twenty-first-century constructs, Western governments are promoting inclusion. For many this means special schools and colleges are joining typical educational settings. The move away from previous traditional thinking has seen the dismantling of specialist provision, distinct roles and a blurring of societal expectation. For example, once children were streamlined for the school that suited their potential; now we have comprehensive schools where every child, no matter what their potential is, is welcome. Although in theory this sounds like a good idea, in practice it means trying to cater for everyone is putting too much pressure upon the system. It also means some individuals will feel like square pegs in round holes!

Social inclusion

Inclusion is a good thing – that is 'exclusion', when it means outlawing or separating some individuals from others, forcibly and against their will, is not good. However, social relating needs to work both ways. Having people understand that an individual might need space and time on their own is not excluding them so much as it is being understanding of their needs. Therefore, being inclusive towards them, means accommodating their changing needs, including allowing for time on their own. On the other hand, inclusive social relationships might mean we need to accommodate the needs of others who might wish us to join in with their activities and not isolate ourselves from them. Finding the balance can be difficult!

The term that defines an individual as autistic implies they have difficulties in certain areas of daily life: social understanding, communication and adaptive thinking. In reality however, there are many individuals, with or without autism, who have difficulties in these areas. Even the 'cool, confident kids' who make it into all manner of successful adult pursuits must fit somewhere into the adult statistics of the one in three divorce rates in our Western society. This suggests that even they, with their social understanding intact, don't always communicate appropriately and don't always meet the expectations of others. This implies that we all have difficulty with social relationships!

So, even though it might be easier to feel 'included' for any student at school who is 'cool', attractive and confident, lots of ordinary individuals, let alone any student with a disability like an autism spectrum disorder (ASD) really struggle to find where they fit in today's society.

Understanding the social rules of any group and knowing how to implement them is crucial to building a sense of being included. But understanding how these change and teaching adaptability to 'difference' is also crucial to successful social relationships.

Social inclusion means finding ways to work with difference.

For those of us with ASD, building successful social relationships will mean several things: understanding one's sensory environment and one's sensory needs (they vary from individual to individual); adapting curriculums, timetables and work schedules to accommodate one's different learning style; providing an environment that is calm, structured, uses natural lighting as far as possible (no fluorescent lights that are a trigger for epilepsy); and making arrangements for lots of one-to-one interaction rather than a permanent group focus.

We each need an environment that welcomes and celebrates who we are, not one that compares and contrasts us to that of others and concludes, 'Because you are not like them you just don't fit'.

Social relationships vary so much between person and person and between situation and situation. For example, the social relationships that exist between classmates often extend to groups of mates that share time and activities together at school but don't meet up outside of school, right through to mates who share at school and outside of school hours too. Having similar interests can be useful if individuals want to share on a social level during and outside of school or work hours. Joining clubs and activities where your mates are is a plus for most of us. But, even though an individual might have a similar interest to an AS individual, it doesn't mean that that they will relate well socially.

Things to consider – scripts

That's typical
'That's typical' I heard her say.
I wondered what she meant?
'You always want it your way'
She echoed without relent.

I waited, silent as a bird,
And pondered on her words.
She just kept talking,
I kept walking,
What was it that I heard?

'I always want it my way?'
What other way could there be?
I only know the proper way,
The way that's there for me.

If we do it her way,
It wouldn't be right at all.
It would be wrong and all along,
I'd know it's wrong and not OK!

So, why can't she understand?
What is it she doesn't get?
I must firmly stand my ground,
I mustn't give in yet!

If I give up she'll never learn.
She'll never know the way.
She calls it 'being stubborn',
But, I'm scripted for this play.

Each of us has our own personality, learning style, interests and belief system. These help to form the person we are today. They also help shape our expectations of ourselves and of others. This, in turn, will directly impact upon our social relationships. The above poem talks about scripts and the things we believe. Each of us is scripted for our lives, but, we also decide what our scripts will tell us and what we will do with this information.

For example: usually families teach their young that we each have responsibilities, to ourselves and to others. We are taught the moral code of 'do to others that which you would have them do to you'. Words like 'should', 'must', 'always', and 'don't' or 'do', are the adjectives used to instil the importance of their instructions. However, if our disposition is one of being literal, black and white, honest and straightforward then we might miss out on appreciating how to adjust our learnings to fit in with social relationships. It's almost automatic for us to expect others to think and feel the same way we do. This can have a negative impact upon other people who might not share our understanding.

ILLUSTRATION OF THIS POINT

In my family each member has their own favourite cup. At my friend's home, however, they don't have favourite cups, so they tend to use whatever cup is clean! Therefore, when my friend comes to my home she might offer to make me a drink and not realize that I like my tea in a particular mug. My being upset with her and believing that she is not being very nice isn't an accurate assessment of her actions. Rather, she is being herself and is behaving as she might if she were in her home. This kind of thing happens all the time in social relationships. So, it's a good idea to be tolerant of people and their different ways of doing things. This helps to build successful social relationships.

BEHAVIOUR

At times, when an individual might not know how to behave socially, they might use 'social avoidance' as a way to cover up their inadequacies. This means they use behaviour (e.g. tantrum, shy away from) to escape or avoid social situations because they are unsure of what is required of them. It is their difficulty with social skills, rather than any sensory difficulty, that is the issue. However, it's not always easy to work this out and, as a matter of course, it's always a good idea to check out sensory issues and eliminate this from the scenario before looking at social skills. Bogdashina (2003) has a checklist in the back of her book to assist with sensory profiling. This is a useful tool. Once this is done and any sensory difficulty is accommodated or ruled out, then Social Stories™ can be explored as a method to help increase the individual's understanding of the situation. Social Stories™ were initially developed by Carol Gray as a tool to help describe a particular social situation and inform the individual of their role within that situation. For example, once informed and aware, an individual is better equipped to work out their role within a social relationship and implement it. See www.thegraycenter.org (accessed 15 January 2008) for further information on Social Stories™.

Social indifference is another behaviour we employ to cover our tracks when we don't know what to do or how to respond in a social situation. We do this by displaying behaviour that neither actively seeks nor obviously avoids social interaction. This behaviour allows us to portray to others a picture that says 'I'm in control' when we actually feel that we are not in control. Again, Social Stories™ and scripting out a role for ourselves can be helpful. These media can simplify and illustrate social interactions, with the aim of increasing understanding of the situation to make it more attractive and more accessible.

Social awkwardness is something that can happen to all of us. As we try to relate our clumsiness of conversation may get in the way of our friendships. The more we try to get it right the less success we have! Sometimes this is due to our having limited interests and not being equipped with enough understanding about the interests of our friends. It can be very helpful to find out what the interests are of the person we want to relate to so that we can share their interests too and not just harp on about our own. Sometimes we can have difficulty with reading and understanding another person's body language so it's hard to work out what the meaning is behind their expressions as well as their words. Rather than risk making inappropriate comments it might be a good idea to check in with them so we can tell what they mean. We can do this by asking such questions as: 'So what are you trying to say?' Or 'So what do you mean by that?' Again, Social Stories™ and scripts illustrating typical scenarios that exist within social relationships can help to provide us with a framework for successful social interaction. They help to paint a picture about various perspectives on the thoughts, emotions and beliefs of others in particular environments, and can offer suggestions for appropriate behaviours and responses.

SOCIAL INTERACTION WITHIN A GROUP

The Group
There were just seven of us,
Seated all around.
The man with the shortest hair
Started to make a sound.
I was quiet.

I wanted to keep watching,
There were Blue Birds in the tree.
The man said something louder,
'Oh, did you speak to me?'
I said

'There are Blue Birds in the tree'
Said I. There was silence in the group.
The man with the shortest hair
Returned to eating his soup.

'There are Blue Birds in the tree',
I stated just once more.
'Wendy, do you want some tea'?
'Do you want me to pour?'
He said.

'There are Blue Birds in the tree'
I only thought this time.
'Why were they not excited'?
'Could they not enjoy this find'?
They all ate soup.

'Wendy, the waiter needs to clear the plates'
The man with the shortest hair spoke.
'Why does this concern me?' I said.
The girl with long hair spoke,
'You need to eat your soup now Wendy,
Hurry up for goodness sakes!'

What had I done?
What did I not get?
The Blue Birds are gone,
I haven't eaten yet.

Reproduced from Lawson, W. (2005) *AS Poetry: Illustrations
from an Aspie Life.* London: Jessica Kingsley Publishers.

The above poem illustrates an occasion when I was so occupied with something I was interested in that my interest took over from that of the group. This wasn't something that I planned to do nor was I being rude and difficult. However, the rest of the group failed to comprehend what was going on for me and I failed to see the situation from the others' point of view.

Let me reiterate a fundamental difference in the design mechanisms for attention between typical individuals and AS individuals. When one's brain is designed to work with single focus (AS individuals) and one isn't so apt at dividing one's attention it is very easy to be occupied with one specific interest. Neurotypical individuals, however, appear to be more at home with lots of different interests and not so focused upon one. Of course they can apply all of their attention to one thing and be fully tuned in to that occupation. But, it seems that their ability to divide their attention enables them to switch topics quickly, swap from one interest to another and even show and share interest in things that don't interest them! This is an asset when it comes to social relationships. On the other hand it's a hindrance when it comes to needing to stay focused on a particular topic (e.g. a university essay) and not be drawn away to some social event (e.g. time at the pub with mates).

So, how do we bridge the gap between us? How do we, as AS individuals, build social relationships that work?

First

The first thing we need to do is understand ourselves and appreciate our strengths. This might be the fact that we are really good at being focused. This single-mindedness makes us candidates for a number of vital traits that build great social relationships. We are loyal, trustworthy, honest, dependable and committed. These are the essential ingredients for the basis of successful social relationships.

Second

The next part of the recipe for successful social relationships is the ability to 'listen' to the other person and put our own 'interest' on hold, for a while. Being listened to, heard and having one's 'needs' accommodated is the hope of every individual. Most people feel that they are not listened to and this can cause an individual to feel uncared for.

Consider the following interactions:

SALLY AND JENNY
Sally would like to relate socially to Jenny but every time she tries it seems like Jenny isn't interested. Sally thinks she might give up on the idea and turn her attentions to other social situations and other potential friends.

The outline below is typical of the interaction, belief systems behind it and the inevitable outcome of the interaction between Jenny and Sally.

What does Sally believe about Jenny?
Each time Sally tries to chat to Jenny, Jenny ignores her and fails to respond to her conversation, therefore Sally believes:

- Jenny is only interested in things Jenny wants to talk about.

- Jenny is not interested in Sally.

- Jenny is selfish.

- Jenny is inconsiderate and rude.

- Jenny would not make a good friend so Sally should look elsewhere for other friends.

JENNY AND SALLY
What does Jenny believe about Sally?

- When Sally talks she always asks lots of questions and she doesn't really wait for Jenny to process the information.

- Sally bombards Jenny with information and questions. She is invasive.

- Therefore, although Jenny would like to be friends it's too difficult. Sally appears to be selfish and Jenny must avoid her.

- If Jenny ignores Sally she will leave her alone and this discomfort will stop.

- Sally is not interested in Jenny. If she were she would stop asking all these questions!

- Jenny has to make Sally go away because she is insensitive and not a nice person.

When one carefully considers the above interaction and beliefs behind it one can see that both of these individuals are wanting to be friends with one another. The problem is in the social skill needed to accommodate the friendship and the beliefs that accompany so much of our social interaction with others.

So, we have stated that social relationships are based upon mutual commitment to the well-being of the other person. For this to happen successfully we each need to learn to listen to what the other is saying. We then need to process this information so we can respond appropriately. Processing words, actions and expectations might take us longer if we are AS individuals, when compared to typical individuals. 'It's perfectly fine to take your time' is one of the rules I use to help me in social situations. The only thing I need to remember is to let the other person know that this is what I'm doing. I might say something like: 'Thanks for sharing that. I'm really interested in what you are saying I just need some time to think that over and then I can respond...' If the other person needs me to answer soon, I might say: 'Just give me a moment to think that over' and, in this way, I'm more likely to answer or respond with care and consideration, rather than make a statement I can't support, don't mean or haven't really understood the implications of.

What are they really saying?

Reading other people's 'body language' is quite a difficult task. Body language is the term used to describe people's non-verbal communication. For example, if a person says 'Yes' but tosses their head, looks away from you or looks down as they speak, it might mean that they are unsure or that they don't mean 'yes' at all. Sometimes people seem to say one thing, but mean another! 'Yeah, right!' could actually mean 'No, I don't think so'. If we are unsure what a person really means we can check in with them and ask. It's better to do this (makes the person think about what they are saying too) than feel misled or misinformed and get upset about that. Some of us work better with words and others understand better when we have a visual image of what someone means. If you are a 'words' person you can use words to your advantage by stating what you have understood back to the person after they have spoken. This gives them a chance to reiterate what they really mean and avoid any misunderstanding!

If you are not a words person but prefer information presented to you in a visual manner (e.g. maps, pictures, posters and cartoons, for example), it's fine to get the person to draw what they mean by literally mapping it out for you or by using photos, video, TV referencing and so on. Many of us find multimedia the greatest tool too. If words take too long to process or they just aren't a comfortable medium for you, then finding alternatives to them, as a way of expressing yourself or as a means to understanding others, is very important.

Communication cards

Communication cards, sometimes referred to as 'autism alert cards', can be useful supplements or replacements for the spoken word.

> I'm too tired to chat just now, please call me later.

They can be used in many situations where socially, the relationship allows for it or where it is a necessary tool in a social relationship to help to keep the relationship healthy. You might have heard the saying 'a picture is like a thousand words' or 'the picture says it all'.

> I'm sorry, forgive me.
> I'd really like to be friends.

> I'm all out of words just now.
> I need a safe place to calm down.
> Please call the person named below. Thank you.
>
> ....

To create these cards you can use your own photos, pictures, drawings and characters. Or, you can simply write your statement onto a card without any pictures, just the words. The point is to be clear and concise about what you wish to communicate and to do so in a timely and respectful way.

Types of social relationships

It's likely that most of our social relationships will be based either around family, friends or colleagues. The flow chart illustrates some of the types of relationships that exist and that we might be part of.

Family $\longrightarrow$ Dad $\longleftrightarrow$ Mum $\longleftrightarrow$ siblings

$\downarrow$

Friends of the family $\longrightarrow$ individual friends $\longleftrightarrow\longleftrightarrow$ individual acquaintances

$\updownarrow$

more intimate friends

Each of our social relationships exists because of genetic link (family) or because of school or work encounters or because we choose to share with someone in a social manner that brings us together to share an interest or a fun encounter. Yet, each of these relationships will be different because they are fostered by individuals with differing personalities, expectations and particular interaction styles. For example, some people you will meet are inclined to greet you with a handshake, whilst others will give you a hug. Some individuals are good at eye contact whilst others look down or away from you when they talk. For some, initiating conversation comes relatively easily whilst, for others, how to begin a conversation and/or how to maintain one, is very difficult. So, our social relationships will vary accordingly.

My friend Katy helped me to understand that social relationships can have many different sides to them. This will mean different relationships bring each of us different experiences. I will use some of Katy's descriptions to illustrate some of the feelings and experiences we might encounter:

Key: different symbols are used to represent the social nature of each relationship type. The symbols provide visual clues. They can be placed against an individual's name, in a flow chart, or diagram, or list. Individuals can also invent their own symbols as ways of separating their friends disposition and relationship to themselves.

O   This symbol represents the type of relationship that is honest and transparent. It reflects so many of our mutual interests and personality traits. Vibrant, alive, fun and trustworthy means this is a social relationship that allows us to be ourselves and to come and go as we feel able. This relationship type might be with a close family member or an intimate friend.

C   This symbol represents a social relationship that one might have with a neighbour, family friend or regular acquaintance. This person has a good heart and can be counted upon to help out when needed. However, they might not be into the thrills and spills of a party life or be interested in adventures.

Q   This symbol might represent a social relationship or friendship that is full of sparkle, glitter and outwardly good times, but sometimes it's hard to get comfortable with this person on an intimate level. Therefore, you might have fun together but would not choose to 'bare your soul' to this person or share very deeply with them.

B   This symbol could represent a social relationship where both parties feel nurtured but where the attachment can get a bit stifling and each person might need time to themselves to recover.

P   This symbol could represent a relationship that appears distant, shallow and defensive. However, with encouragement and opportunity to share and work together on projects, this type of relationship could prove enlightening and fruitful.

R   This social relationship is composed of friends who hang out together and enjoy being seen to be fashionable and 'cool'. However, it's not the type of relationship that stays still for long, is always on the move and is only interested in superficial communication.

U This symbol represents the type of social relationship that is pretty much an 'all rounder'. It's solid, dependable, open, trustworthy, loving, committed and unconditional.

M This symbol could represent the type of social relationship that might seem odd and a bit different. Although it fosters support, kindness and is very loyal, there are none of the trappings of fashion or culture to limit its conventions. Others may see this relationship as 'earthy', rough or 'hippie' in nature.

The types of relationships outlined above might seem familiar to you, or they might not. You might have one or two of these in your life at any one time. It's very likely that you will experience these from time to time with your changing situations. The important thing to remember is that no one type of social relationship will meet all of your social needs. Rather, each of us needs a smattering of each!

For some of us, face-to-face meeting and the lack of enough processing time are major deterrents to developing social contacts and, therefore, to building social relationships. With the advance of internet and mobile phone technology, we can now move on past these obstacles. A useful resource for websites that access other AS information and chat sites is: www.dragonsplace.co.uk/information.html (accessed 7 September 2007).

The above chapter is only a beginning to understanding and enjoying successful social relationships. It aims to help us understand that social relationships are difficult for us all and they take time and effort to work out. The good news is therefore, with practice and application we each can have successful social relationships.

Bibliography

Bogdashina, O. (2003) *Sensory Perceptual Issues in Autism and Asperger Syndrome.* London: Jessica Kingsley Publishers.

Lawson, W. (2001) *Understanding and Working with the Spectrum of Autism: An Insider's View.* London: Jessica Kingsley Publishers.

Lawson, W. (2003) *Build Your Own Life: A Self-Help Guide To Asperger's Syndrome.* London: Jessica Kingsley Publishers.

Lawson, W. (2005) *Friendships the Aspie Way.* London: Jessica Kingsley Publishers.

Chapter 10: Socializing 101 for Aspies

Liane Holliday-Willey

Introduction by Luke Beardon

Liane is an excellent communicator through the written word and this is another example of her expressive language skills. She also provides a way in which social skills can be developed which may prove beneficial to many individuals. One thing of interest is the concept of perception, particularly self-perception. Liane gives the example of having had a bad experience socially – although others may feel that the experience was not as bad as she thinks. Two very important points here; one, NTs should never patronize the individual with an 'I know better' attitude. I have often observed people saying things like 'Don't worry so much, there's nothing for you to worry about', when clearly the worry is a very real issue for the individual. Second, I think it is an excellent concept to teach that although a situation has been stressful or negative for the individual, the perceptions of others may be very different. So, even though the individual with AS may believe an experience has gone badly because of how they feel, the reality for others in the experience may be much more positive. By teaching this directly to people with AS it may be that individuals will be less self-critical and develop more confidence and self-esteem.

Watch a National Geographic special or spend some time at a local zoo and you'll soon discover that most mammals are social creatures. Watch closely and you'll see socializing is both an art learned very early on through role modelling and, yes, trial and error. Most humans are born with a neurological system that is wired with the desire to socialize, and most are also wired to be very receptive to the learning process involved. Lucky them.

Some of you might be thinking, 'Is it really possible for someone with AS to learn how to socialize?' Happily, it is. We with autism spectrum disorders (ASDs) can learn how to socialize through observing skilled and accomplished role models, and by learning the rudimentary pieces of socializing. This chapter provides the template that I personally used to help me learn the social game. In order to make the ideas work for others, you should feel free to customize the ideas to fit the Aspie as much as possible. As you read this chapter, note that it is based on the assumption that those who read it have a desire to socialize, for it is true, not everyone on this planet does!

Step one: Build an understanding of the concept and rules of socializing

My father, a card-carrying Aspie, has virtually no desire to socialize. One of his favourite quotes is, 'I see no desire in socializing because I rarely learn anything when I do. So, why waste my time?' Dad has a solid point as long as the premise to socializing is to learn. And herein lies a subtle but essential point – the concept of socializing is really up for debate, at least among those with AS. To Dad, it is about learning. To some, it is about making contacts that will make career advancement a reality. To my teenager, socializing is about hanging out with friends doing nothing more than watching a movie together. According to the Encarta® World English Dictionary socializing is about *relating* to the *people* and *systems* in a society *in a friendly and mutually satisfactory way.* Say what? This concept confuses the logic right out of me. Granted, I am a linguist so I have a penchant toward taking apart semantics, but in this case – wow! I am hung up on every word in italics. What does it mean to 'relate'? For me, it means talking about my favourite interests or passions with those who share those same interests and passions. Beyond that, 'relate' means nothing tangible to me. What does 'people and systems' mean? What people? All people? Even those I do not agree with or understand or enjoy? What systems? Political? Religious? Academic? Neighbourhood cliques? All of the above? Is that even possible? How can I be all things to every one in every situation? Nope. That is impossible. And what of 'in a friendly and mutually satisfactory way?' I think friendly is when people smile and then leave me alone never asking me for a favour or cutting in front of me while I am in a queue. Imagine my surprise when I am told friends should want to do favours for others. Do not get me wrong, I'll help others when they need me to, but it better be a need and not a whimsical want. There are few things more annoying to me than someone who asks me for favours they are perfectly competent to do on their own. Does this mean I am not friendly? I would never cut in line. I would never wish anyone harm. I would never smash my car into a parked car and not report my contact information to the owner. Seems to me I am very friendly. But I digress... 'Mutually satisfactory?' You're kidding. How often is it really possible for everyone involved in a group to be mutually satisfied with the way the group is going? Listen in on Parliament, Congress or siblings to hear my point proven loud and clear.

The concept of socializing is hard for an Aspie like me, but I have been able to do a reasonably good job of learning how to socialize in a way that is for the most part, acceptable. I have long ago given up thinking I will ever be the kind of gal who can waltz seamlessly through a social event with nothing but good graces left in my wake. I will forever make a miscue or commit a faux pas that will no doubt sting and possibly even stain my heart, but so be it. So what. As my dad used to say, 'If your mistakes aren't going to kill you, they can't be that bad.' Good point!

Creatures have been manning together in pods or communities likely since we first came into existence. This seems to be an important part of our survival as species, far beyond that of simply people who enjoy the company of others. In fact, medical doctors find that human touch can prolong life and hasten the healing process. So, too, does laughter heal the heart and body. Sure, animals and funny books can serve as good second-place replacements to human interaction, but the bottom line is: humans seem to have been meant to socialize to at least some degree, to what degree is individual. When helping an Aspie learn to socialize take care that you do not superimpose your thoughts on socializing norms, on to the Aspie's expectations and/or needs when it comes to their sharing time with others. But do try to make the case in point to the Aspie, which is: everyone has to interact with others at some point, so the experience might as well be a happy and successful one!

I learned the hard way that there are certain socializing rules everyone needs to master, at least to some degree. I am told neurotypical people learn these rules very easily, and without much direct teaching, but I am not at all convinced people with AS will pick up on these rules so easily. As such, I recommend counsellors directly discuss with their Aspie client the rules of socializing below, for without an understanding of these typical social rules, we will be bound for failure...

Successful socializing requires the ability to:

- politely enter and exit the conversations of others as they are going on
- 'read' others accurately
- consider other people's points of view and not just your own
- establish common interest points to discuss
- make others feel at ease by not arguing with them or criticizing their points of view
- understand how to begin conversations in a way that includes others and elicits others' returned conversations
- know what topics are typically off limits: religion, politics and personal health issues are good examples of things most people would rather not discuss
- control emotions so they do not dominate a conversation, nor create discomfort in others
- make good eye-contact and keep personal space to a proper distance.

After you are convinced the Aspie you are working with understands the global concept of socializing and the general rules one must adhere to when meeting with others, it will be time to provide the more specific lessons and tips which follow.

Step two: The five Ws

Once a person understands the rules of good socializing, it is time to start providing good learning opportunities for watching examples of success-ful socializing. For example, simply watching a video, DVD or TV show of a well-contrived social scene, may be something the Aspie can readily relate to, especially if it is a videotape that shows people socializing around an activity or topic the Aspie personally enjoys. I, for example, would enjoy watching people engaging in conversation or activity spent around horses. But show me a tape spent around people who are talking about the history of wars, and I'll either go to sleep or wander off to another activity or daydream. While I completely support the use of media as a teaching tool, I am also an avid believer in field trip experiences, believing they are the real tricks of the trade if anxieties about being out of the comfort zone can be controlled. Provided the person with AS is fine with going out and about to learn things, I'd suggest taking them to a situation where they can actually observe real socializing. Observe, not participate in – yet. The emphasis at this point is on observing and learning, not application. So, gather the Aspie and take them to an event where they can see others enjoying time together. My father and I used to go to airports and shopping malls to watch people interacting. We also watched folks at the restaurant we regularly attended, commenting as we watched on their demeanour, word choice and suspected relationship with one another. I often wonder if we weren't thought of as rude or impolite, so obvious was our staring! When I became a mother, I chose to take my daughters to Renaissance festivals where interactions were largely staged and completely other-era-based, yet, where it was possible to openly stare and watch human conversation and behaviour. Other such opportunities abound and again, if there is a way to incorporate the Aspie's favourite topic in the lesson, the better the results are likely to be. I like history, so Renaissance festivals were a natural for me, just as horse shows or architectural tours would be.

Before engaging in one of the observation activities, I suggest you provide the Aspie with a study sheet intended to keep them on task and tuned in to the purpose of the experience, and to help them stay alert for things they might not normally be aware of (such as facial expressions, non-verbal language, vocal prosody, etc.). For example, you could write up something like the following:

> Watching the behaviour of others is a great way to learn how to act yourself! Actors and actresses, parents in parenting classes, attorneys learning from judges – all sorts of people in all sorts of professions look toward others as suitable role models for teaching them how to behave in any given situation. Today, we're going to watch a video [or observe at a horse show, etc.]. Please use this handout to help you focus on what you are watching. Feel free to write down your thoughts and to talk to me at any time during this exercise, but do try to keep your thoughts

and comments on-task. That is, keep them related to what you are observing, not about something else you'd rather be doing or seeing.

Pretend you are a journalist who is trained to answer the five Ws in their writing – the **who**, **what**, **when**, **where** and **how** – (the idea being once these essential facts are answered for, the story will be accurate and complete) and ask yourself the following types of questions when making your observations.

Who is engaged in the conversation?

What kind of conversation does it appear to be? Happy, serious, silly, business only, etc.

When do the participants break in to the conversation with their own thoughts? Is it after someone else finishes their statement? Or are people speaking all at once?

Where is this socializing taking place? Is it a public place like a grocery store? Is it at a festive place like a sporting event or behind closed doors, say in a car where no one could possibly hear them?

How are the participants behaving? How close are they standing in relation to one another? Are they looking at one another when they talk? Or are they looking down at their feet or off to the side? Are they whispering and acting as if they do not want anyone else to hear them? Are they speaking very loudly as if to invite the world to hear and join in?

Once you've made all these observations, try to determine what kinds of patterns people who socialize make. Can you make generalizations about gender and age? Do older people tend to be more reserved and young children louder and more animated? When people are in public, do they talk about things that seem vague or bland, or do they talk about very personal things such as politics or religion?

After you have made your determinations, try to summarize your findings into a schema you can use as you continue to develop your social skills. Call this schema your five Ws.

Caregivers, please note that such a worksheet could be used several times until the person with AS has truly found a way to incorporate the necessary learning into their schema. And eventually, it should be enough to simply remind the person with AS to *think of the five Ws* when next they engage in a new social situation, as just that cue should be enough for them to bring up all the background skills they have learned during this process.

Step three: Build confidence

Negative social experiences can be paralysing. Just one really bad evening with others can send someone into the safe confines of their own home, for a very long time if not forever. I should know. I have spent months on end refusing to be part of a social function following what I perceived to be a bad, bad experience. Eventually, I learned that my perception was not usually what others held as the truth. I tend to be very hard on myself and I tend to inflate the reality of a bad situation, if it is 'my' situation. I have no problem giving others the benefit of the doubt and no problem overlooking their problems, but boy am I tough on myself when I feel I have acted in error or made a fool of myself. I remember being at a party with a group of couples I felt were friends of my husband's and mine. I thought things were going smoothly but, before too long, I overheard a gaggle of women talking about me. They were questioning how my husband could be with someone who was as 'odd as Liane'. They were quite outspoken about how hyper I was and how loud and obnoxious. Looking back, I should have left this experience telling myself that bad social skills aren't something only we with AS struggle with but, sadly, I came away wondering what in the world I had done that was so odd, loud and obnoxious. This experience plagued me for a very long time and was in fact the main reason behind my husband and me leaving the entire town and moving to a state ten hours away.

I think if I did not have children I may have spent the rest of my life hiding from almost every social engagement, but the kids' social life encouraged me to be the best socializer I could be. Simply put, I was absolutely determined not to let my shortcomings as a conversationalist or party guest interfere with my ability to conduct myself properly at my kids' school parties and after school festivities. It hurts me to admit I could not muster the courage or strength to become a decent socializer for my own benefit, but I suppose the fact that I was able to learn how to socialize, should be enough for my psyche to embrace. I do know that I now have more confidence than I did ten years ago, and more than I had ten months ago.

Aspies need to begin the 'how to socialize' process believing in their self and in the positive. It is terribly difficult to believe in one's self-worth if one has been criticized, ridiculed, bullied or left out for years on end. The key is to convince the Aspie to take back their power and their future. A wise friend of mine tells me to beware of the self-fulfilling prophecy: if you think it will happen it will. If the Aspie believes they will never have what it takes to socialize, they won't. I suggest a course or lecture in cognitive restructuring to help the person with AS reprogram how he sees himself (see Attwood 1999). Without a healthy dose of strong self-confidence, it's unlikely the Aspie will continue to try and improve their social skills. I cannot over-emphasize that point.

As tempted as you might be, resist the urge to build confidence by downplaying the difficulties inherent for Aspies learning how to socialize. Statements like, 'This isn't that hard', or 'Anyone can do this', sound innocuous enough, but they really do not serve to make any of us feel better. To the contrary, they can make us feel as if we are silly or inept if we aren't in fact able to find social success. Confidence comes with honest and objective counselling. Use that truth with the Aspies you assist, and you will not go wrong.

Step four: Practice makes perfect

There is an old joke: a man asks a woman in the city of New York, 'How do I get to the great musician's performance theatre called Carnegie Hall?' The woman replies, 'Practice, practice, practice.' Like most Aspies, I enjoy this joke because it is a play on words, but also because it is so true – practice is the key to everything; practice makes perfect.

I grew up doing a lot of thespian activities. I did very well in the acting world. It was easy for me to copy the actions of those I saw and easy enough for me to become someone else. All I needed to do was watch a character on TV, or a person in real life (for example, a waitress if I was to play a waitress in a play), in order to make myself into that character. The key, however, to maintaining that character, was to practise it over and over and over. I tended to practise in front of a full-length mirror, taking note of everything I could from my mannerisms to my facial expressions. And when I really wanted to perfect my facial expressions, I would practise in front of a mirror that only showed me from my head to my shoulders. I would also practise my vocal qualities including my prosody, inflections, rate, etc., on a tape recorder. Like any good thespian, I also did my fair share of practising before a group. My fellow actors were very good at critiquing my ability to transform myself into someone new. The same ideas for acting a part, should easily translate to acting as a good social being.

Using whatever metaphor works well for the Aspie under your guidance, encourage the philosophy of practice makes perfect and then set about designing opportunities that promote solid and successful practice. In addition to the ideas listed above, you could suggest the Aspie:

- Role-plays good social skills among family members who are happy and able to play along. Let the Aspie set the criteria and roles for the socialize situation (a party scenario, a job interview, etc.) and then ask that the family members take on the roles (the boss, the party hostess, etc.) of those who would be involved in the scenario were it real life. Do this with as many social scenarios as possible and while doing so, help the Aspie to realize there are subtle and not-so-subtle differences in how one is to behave towards someone in authority, someone they have a personal attraction toward, a casual friend, a new friend, etc.

- Memorize the common interpretations of most non-verbal cues. This is so important for people with AS because we cannot read emotions, facial expressions or body language very well, if at all. I took several classes in non-verbal communications during college and I'll never forget the 'ah ha' moments I experienced each time I learned a new cue. A good book on non-verbal communication might be all the Aspie needs, or perhaps they will only need a list or lecture from you regarding the meanings of the most typical body language, appearance and sounds (groans, sighs, etc.).

- Memorize affect signs as best as possible. This is a grey area for many of us and it is important to realize that even the best people-readers will misconstrue emotions from time to time. Just ask any man why his wife is crying and you will see that point proved! But there are generalizations people with AS can learn. Tears, for example, tend to mean sadness. They can, however, mean great joy. When you help someone with AS come to terms with affect signs, remind them that the context of the conversation itself will help them figure out what the affect signs are implying. If someone is crying while talking about their dog getting hit by a car, for example, it is safe to bet the tears mean sadness. Whereas a person crying while talking about a joke they heard is likely to mean the tears are happy tears.

- Memorize and learn what various trendy sayings and idioms mean, but take care to know exactly who can use that kind of specific language. For example, people of one geographic area or ethnicity can call others in their same group certain words that others outside of the group should not.

- Learn to identify what kinds of language and behaviours are appropriate to what kinds of situations and which people. For example, the way a person speaks to his new and conservative boss is far different from the way a person would speak to his long-time friend and co-worker. This is a very difficult task to learn and should it seem impossible for the person with AS, it might well be time to discuss disclosure and when/whom to disclose to.

Step five: Evaluate the experience

Self-awareness can be very difficult for people with AS. Metacognition and self-awareness skills are not something that comes easy to many people, but particularly people who lack strong theory-of-mind abilities. The only way I have been able to think about who I am and what I am doing is by looking at myself academically and logically. In other words, I have learned how to figure myself out much like a mathematician learns how to figure out a complex numerical problem. It can be very difficult to objectively evaluate any personal journey. Accordingly, it is my suggestion that others help the Aspie evaluate how they behaved. To this day, I routinely repeat or even act out for one of my family members or closest friends, how I behaved. I try to re-create the scene as accurately as possible, relying on my strong echolalia skills to act the part of everyone involved in the scene. I become each of the people present in the group I was interacting with and when I have completed the situation I felt went poorly, I ask my helper to let me know where I messed up, what social cues I missed and what I might do to improve my abilities.

While I largely rely on my family members and peers to help me with social learning, I do try to evaluate my performance on my own, too. I ask myself questions that are tied in to the definition of good socializing:

- Was my part of the socializing connected to the others' conversation?

- Did I stay on the topic at hand or did I bring up my favourite topics?

- Did I blurt out anything embarrassing or inappropriate?

- Did I talk over other people, speaking at the same time they did, or did I wait my turn and then speak?

- Did I make proper eye contact or did I stare for too long or look away too often?

- Did I fidget or rub my hands or stem in any way?

- Was my voice monotonous or did I manage to use inflection and rate changes properly?

- Did I stand too close or too far away from others in the group?

- Did I have fun and laugh and enjoy myself? Or was the event just too much of a struggle for me? And if so, what can I do to avoid future struggles?

While my self-questioning is designed to address my personal issues with socializing, they are rather common for most with AS. Feel free to suggest the Aspie you are helping employ these questions and add others that are precisely well matched for their personal struggles.

Every day it becomes easier to put myself out on a social limb. I have managed to figure out how I react to the pitfalls and challenges of socializing. I can almost always predict what kinds of situations will make me excessively nervous and if there is one thing I try very hard to guard against, it is a big social fall brought on by excessive nerves! When trying to access if I am dangerously perched too close to falling off the social limb, I evaluate my physical responses. For example, I study my breathing and my pulse rate. I listen for the loudness of my speech and the rate at which I am speaking. I check to make sure I am breathing (did you know many of we Aspies with anxiety issues forget to breathe?) If red flags go off during my self-evaluation…if my pulse rate is too high, I am speaking too loudly or too fast, if I am holding my breath…I know I am in trouble of disappearing into my empty zone. To lessen the effects of my social anxiety, I rely on biofeedback and my peers who help to calm me down by reassuring me or whispering little social behaviour hints during my struggles.

I used to push myself to at least try new social opportunities, believing that I would someday shed all my AS and come out a shiny neurotypical who could laugh and enjoy life among the rest of the world, without so much as a hiccup. I do not expect that much of myself any more. I have come to accept the fact that as close to neurotypical as I now am, I will never completely erase all my AS traits. I am more than fine with that reality. I even often wish I still possessed some of my more endearing AS traits that were washed away in my desire to fit in. Lately, I have begun to give myself permission to skip social events, telling myself it is OK to not attend every party or event, not even the small ones I could likely handle well enough. Simply put, I am learning to accept my limitations without regrets. And when I do turn down an invitation or refuse to go to an event, I provide myself with a little reward – more time alone! Yes, I have learned how to socialize better than my parents ever thought I would, but when all is said and done, I would still rather spend time with a good book or my computer or my horse and kids. And if you ask me, there is nothing wrong with that!

Bibliography

Attwood, T. (1999) 'Modifications to Cognitive Behaviour Therapy to Accommodate the Cognitive Profile of People with Asperger's Syndrome.' Available at www.cabinetoffice.gov.uk/strategy/stomach2.pdf. Accessed 23 october 2007.

Chapter 11: Making Friends is Not Easy

PJ Hughes

Introduction by Luke Beardon

PJ mentions in this chapter the question I put to him one day regarding why he liked me. I am always fascinated to ask my friends with AS this question, and more fascinated and interested in the diversity of answers. One thing that NTs should always bear in mind is that the concept of friendship may well differ from one person to the next. Two commonalities I have noted are how well the friend understands the individual – this often includes having some understanding of AS – and the sharing of a special interest. The former commonality seems similar to NT relationships, where mutual understanding is seen as a strong factor in developing and maintaining relationships. The second commonality is also seen in NT relationships, though is less important I believe than to those with AS. What this highlights is the fact that NTs should not try to support individuals with AS to have relationships that fulfil simply NT concepts, but should afford respect for the AS way of thinking – after all, it is the relationship that is important, not just what it is based on. As PJ once said to me, very poignantly, regarding 'normal' behaviour: 'My behaviour is perfectly normal to me, it is others that I find strange!'

Introduction

I was diagnosed with Asperger Syndrome in July 1999 and this was by complete accident. This is because my father was doing a ceiling job in a

London hospital and was talking to one of the psychologists about me. It would seem apparent that the psychologist was asking relevant questions and then gave suitable directions for a diagnosis.

One of the things I find difficult is making friends. There are many reasons for this. In fact, my friends seem to stay very much in the arena in which I know them and they don't often spill over into other arenas, such as going to the pub or 'hanging out' generally. That is not to say it doesn't happen. I have noted that I tend to be with other people socially in short bursts, i.e. for a couple of hours or so at a time. This tends to suit me because I am more naturally a loner and being with others for significant lengths of time can create anxiety and distress for me. In fact, these friendships may well be best described in other ways. This is because I would define these types of friendships in a different way. Could they be better described as acquaintances or as something in between? To be honest, I don't really know. It could be said that, like any form of relationship, there are those I get on with and those I don't. There will almost certainly be some that fall in the middle. I have my own ideas what friends are, but the ones I have don't seem to particularly fit into this category.

In order to describe friendship, one would have to define what friends are. Attwood (1998) also considers this issue. The answer isn't a simple one, especially if one looks at the bigger picture such as when thinking about the circle of friends, acquaintances and so on. I believe that I would be in the right area if I described some of the factors involved in friendship included getting on with (and being nice to) each other, having certain forms of communication and discussion and being willing to compromise; or certainly something to this effect. There is also taking part in activities together and these shared activities are made easier if there are other people sharing the common goal. I also think that there are different levels of liking other people, which is partly why the circle of friends exists, at least in part. This leads on to a concentric circle picture of interpersonal space. Roughly speaking, this starts with oneself, i.e. mind and body, right through to somebody else's space, again mind and body. In between are other spaces, such as those where one feels safe and secure, personal territory, shared space and so on.

I have had numerous meetings with Luke Beardon, a senior lecturer at the Autism Centre at Sheffield Hallam University, while I was writing a book. This chapter was going to be a dual authorship, but other things got in the way so I ended up writing it by myself with Luke helping with the editing. During one of these meetings, he asked me why I liked him. I remember that his face was looking away from me at the time. Part of the answer was that he had an understanding of the autistic spectrum. Often, I feel, this is useful, but I don't think it always is. I believe there are other factors involved. It usually takes me quite a time to get used to people, which makes it a bit more difficult to form friendships. There are some exceptions. These have sometimes led to fruitful friendships. Furthermore, there is what I call a 'trust zone'. There are very few people in this zone. This is because they have to truly earn my trust in many things. At this point in time I am not in a position to define them, as they are difficult to explain, although an almighty understanding of the autistic spectrum is part of the equation. To be honest, and no offence to my family, my family don't yet fit this criteria. But they do fit totally different criteria. Generally speaking, it does take me a while to get used to people. This means that forming friendships is not easy. Similarly, it also takes some time before I could call someone a friend.

In this chapter, I shall demonstrate how difficult forming friendships is for me, particularly through the description just given. Many things are important for me and I would probably describe myself, in some way, quite obviously egocentric. In actual fact, I am probably no more egocentric, or selfish, for that matter, than anyone else. The problem is how this is portrayed.

History

Looking back over my life, I have noticed that friendships seem to have been fairly short-lived, with pigeonholed life spans. I haven't kept in touch with anyone I was at school with, but have remained in sporadic contact with two, maybe three, people I was an undergraduate at university with. In fact, apart from long-standing family friends (mainly as a result of my parents, in particular) I have generally not kept in contact with anyone from my childhood years. On the whole, my closest friends are often kept at arm's length because friendships are rarely close for me. My friendships are based in four main areas: sport and associated activities, languages and associated activities, education, and activities relating to the autistic spectrum.

I have played numerous sports over my life, usually categorized under dangerous sports. The sports I played during my school years were cricket, martial arts (judo and Shaolin kung fu), rugby union, soccer and swimming. At university, I have undertaken martial arts (Hung Kuen kung fu and jujitsu) and rugby league. Since then I have dabbled in tai chi chuan (I have so far studied three styles), running and weightlifting. The present forms of exercises I am doing are tai chi (I am currently studying the Wu style, I have previously studied the Yang and Lee styles) and walking. Most of the places I go to at the moment, such as work, are within walking distance.

My main non-sporting interest is foreign languages, particularly Italian and Spanish. I have been learning and developing them through a mixture of evening classes and language clubs. I go to the former, depending on what is available and the latter when I can, although the Spanish club doesn't exist at the moment. Another avenue I am currently looking for is a tandem-learning partner, which is where two people of different native languages with an interest in the other meet up and practise their language skills with each other. I am also looking for a suitable penpal in both Italian and Spanish.

Since I got diagnosed, I have undertaken various part-time courses at college and university. The thing is that most of the courses I do are for my own enjoyment so I don't have the pressure of proving myself. The only exception is anything related to autism, more of which later. I am currently studying languages, which I have just written about. I have obtained grade A at GCSE in both Italian and Spanish in a year of studying them. I also have got through the OCN (Open College Network) year 5 in both these languages, which are OCN level 3. I also did A-levels in film studies and music, getting grade C in both. Doing such activities does help in some way in making friends and acquaintances. Often, the latter is the stronger of the two categories.

Autism itself is a passion of mine. Looking at the subject in general, it would not be surprising that this is the case because passions such as this are part and parcel of the condition. There are courses on the subject. They can come up as individual units on degrees such as psychology. Others are postgraduate courses (in the autistic spectrum itself). There are two forms of this. In a taught form, there are master's courses for the non-scientists, such as for support workers. There are research degrees for pretty much any related area. Currently, I have a Postgraduate Certificate in Asperger Syndrome. I am looking to progress onto the master's degree, the only hurdle being finance. I am also looking at the science side as well because I shall then have grounding in the three main areas of the condition. Whenever I can, I try and attend the Asperger Social Group in Sheffield. We meet every so often and socialize. We have gone bowling, gone to the cinema and have met in a pub, amongst other activities.

So, in effect, throughout my post-diagnosis education I have met people and have made, at some level, friends, at some (probably low) level with certainly some of them. As to whether there'll be anything long term, time will tell. A lot of my work on autism will make me known to others and vice versa. It could be prudent to make note of business friends, which are those who become friends for work/ambition reasons. I make note of the word 'networking' at this point because this may be considered a form of friendship.

There are also a number of things that I do alone. To be honest, this is the area that is most natural to me. I am a big fan of both film and music. I go to the cinema every week without fail, wherever possible. I have been known to see two, maybe three, films on the same day. Having said that, I have also been involved in radio and have had radio shows on a couple of student radio stations and I have been involved behind the scenes of a third. Additionally, my chores (shopping, housework etc.) are very much a solo activity and are often done as part of a routine.

I do go to pubs and nightclubs from time to time. While I was at university, going to the Student Union on a Friday night was a regular occurrence when I was an undergraduate and I do go to meet friends occasionally in a pub in Sheffield now and again. I did go to rock music nightclubs a few times when I was at a previous job. This form of meeting friends is not a current standard practice for me. Also at university, I appeared in several stage productions with the university drama society. After a 15-year or so gap, I am hoping to get back on stage. This will I hope include my other interest in music as I am also a guitarist and clarinettist; so, all going well, I shall be back a performer. I have been to see a Led Zeppelin tribute band, called Letz Zep, on several occasions with a friend from an Italian class.

There are also very rare friendships amongst work colleagues for me in the sense of spilling over into my personal life, but this is something that I generally prefer to be kept separate. I don't mean anything offensive about this, but I often prefer to keep work and leisure separate. I have gained work-related friendships through my roles in the disability groups I am with, i.e. the disability sub-group in Sheffield and Civil Service Disablity Support network.

What type of friendship would I like?

The honest answer, at the moment, is probably a rather muddled one. There are times when I want to be with people more regularly. There are other times when I want to be alone. Often it is easier to be with others for short periods. This is probably why I find having friends in a pigeonhole format, with no intent for causing offence, more comfortable and natural. It is also a frustrating one. I have had moments when I wanted friendship, but such feelings have generally faded away. The reason, I suppose, is because making friends is generally difficult. The types of hobbies I am doing I find satisfying which makes me happy. There have been times, however, that I would have liked to develop and create friendships, but have not really been sure how to do so. This has been frustrating and it has sometimes shown. For me, this has been because of not really knowing or understanding properly what to do.

I am aware of befriending schemes for individuals on the autistic spectrum. While this is a great idea, it doesn't appeal to me personally. This is because I have other interests and have a preference to be alone. There are, however, exceptions and variations in my own case. As I have written earlier, I am looking at my own variations on this. I have already written about looking for tandem-learning partners and penpals in the foreign languages I have already been learning, which are Italian and Spanish. To date, there has been no real success, but I am still trying. It could be argued that this is my part in the individual nature of the autistic spectrum.

I do strongly believe that befriending schemes are important and useful in whatever form they take. I also think they have to be used sensibly and wisely. This is not just for personal safety but also for whether it is useful for the individual concerned. There is a seeming sense of ambiguity in autism. I know of situations where individuals are highly socially active, even though there is an interpretation of a sense of oddness by other people. There are those who would love to form friendships, but find it difficult. In both cases there is, and has been, a danger of being socially excluded. This, in my own way, has been the case for me. This is where such befriending schemes are brilliant. There are also who those want (or prefer) to be left alone, even though there are other individuals (such as family) who would like them to have friends. My belief on the last group is simply this. Why should anyone be forced or encouraged to have friends? I acknowledge that social skills can be (or are) useful in certain situations such as jobs etc., but these are best left to the pertinent situations.

General thoughts

One of the ladies I know who, at the time of writing, has been supporting me in Sheffield, set up a pastime activity group. This is fairly similar to the various autism social groups in set up. She approached me for a few ideas from my own experiences. This is a good idea because it gets the proverbial ball rolling to undertake social activities because social interaction may not be a 'natural process' for us. The activity is gone through in detail from what activity is done, such as going bowling, through to what to wear, travel to and from the venue, finances etc. Admittedly, this is not really useful for me because of the activities I am already undertaking, but it is useful for motivating others in becoming socially active if they so desire. Of course, the autistic spectrum is a very individual one! This is probably why my input has been useful because I have much experience and, hopefully, this will be of use to others. There are also other groups that involve social activities and are usually linked in some way to the National Autistic Society. My belief is that any groups that help in social techniques are useful for those who want to develop such skills.

Retrospectively, I have been encouraged to develop social skills throughout my life. The problem is that I don't always want or need them. I have already touched upon this previously in general terms. The question is: for whose benefit are they (i.e. for parents/whatever or the individual)? If an individual doesn't want to make friends, why force it? If the individual does want to make friends, how can they be encouraged and in what form? For example, if an individual likes, say, cricket (or, indeed, any other sport or whatever) how can friendships spring from this? Playing the sport, or whatever, may not work, but going and watching may. I cannot stress enough how individualistic such situations are. Ultimately, the truth is the happiness of the individual on the autistic spectrum. If they are happy to be alone, then so be it. If they are looking for friendship, then it will be worth looking at the types of things that will work. I have already given one or two ideas on this.

There is quite a bit of my experience in social interaction which I place under accidental management. This is because I realized that my social skills were not exactly like other people's, so I undertook activities that I felt might help, given my lack of understanding of the autistic spectrum at the time even though it wasn't natural for me. I am referring to techniques I have employed accidentally without realizing their importance. I have already mentioned them previously. They are being involved with the drama society, radio and Rugby League at university and being in the Territorial Army for nine years. If I knew I had Asperger Syndrome at the time, these activities may well have been different. Since my diagnosis, many questions have been answered. This goes for many situations in my life.

Earlier, I alluded to my obsession in autism. I do believe that such obsessions can lead to many fruitful lives, such as friendship and employment. This is why such obsessions could be used as a basis to form friendships. For example, I have already mentioned interest in languages. This is why I am looking for penpals and tandem-learning partners.

A follow-up to this would be marriage and children. This is like friendship for me, it has depended what point of time as to whether I would like this or not. Finding the right lady is hard enough, without having to worry about getting married and having kids! Social situations, in general, can pose so many hazards that developing in-depth social groups may prove tough-going. I am not saying they cannot happen, but they could be different from a standard, mainstream understanding of what they are.

At a personal level, I have a need for security and territory. This is where I have naturally defined the boundaries where I basically feel safe. I have consequently developed trust and comfort zones. To get into these zones does take time and effort. Yet, the friendships I have developed, without intending offence, seem to be more acquaintances than 'proper' friendships.

During my Postgraduate Certificate in Asperger Syndrome, I wrote about potential problems posed by the condition in social situations. In this assignment, there is a distinct overlap with forming friends because there is a huge amount to consider when socialising. There are, in all likelihood, going to be other issues involved. After all, certain lights and sounds could prove problematic for an individual on the autistic spectrum. I have, particularly as a child, been concerned by thunderstorms and barking dogs. Hence, sensory issues can be a very real hazard. There are some examples given in the film *Rain Man* (Levinson 1988). Whilst this film may be fictional, the example, in my view, is still useful. For example, when the fire alarm sounds when Raymond is cooking something at the end of the film. Compare this to the music played in pubs and consider how disturbing this could be. Similarly, when Raymond dances with his brother's girlfriend in the lift and he says her kiss is wet. Whilst this situation is something I found amusing, there are very real problems with interpersonal contact. Furthermore, while I think the film is a handy reference on the condition, it is only an example of the condition, not a general overview. I cannot stress this enough, even in my lectures/speeches/talks/whatever, I am the same, merely an example. There is absolutely no such thing as being representative or typical of the condition I'm afraid.

Altogether, even with the general description of friendship, it is not an easy job making friends and keeping them. For me, it is also how I know them as they seldom slip over into other areas in my life. It sometimes annoys me that I feel I have to continually work things out socially. Similarly, I think there are exceptions as well. It is just spotting them. Other factors can be irritating too. Routines, for example, can drive me berserk when I am talking to a lady I have taken a fancy to! This is because I feel two paths opening up as well as the ambiguity and, therefore, panic grips me.

Have there been any potential friendships that I may have missed? The answer to this is quite probably. Looking back over my life there have probably been two or three occasions where I have realised that I was being chatted up in some form or other. The annoying thing was that I missed them at the time.

What about birthdays and Christmases? I remember, as a child, I did have birthday parties and did things socially at Christmas. As I have grown older, Christmas has become quite depressing because of social interaction overload and I try to keep this period as quiet as possible. For a long, long time, birthday celebrations fell out of favour. More recently, I have invited a fairly small number of friends to go out for a meal. So far it has been at the same restaurant at the same time where I have invited the same, so far, friends. At the moment, it has been at 1430 hours on the Saturday before my birthday. I was born in October 1968. I guess that it would be a possibility that I could have a more significant gathering when I am 40 (I could do something similar for each subsequent decade), but I have not thought about that yet as it is rather early to think about it.

What hazards do I face in forming friends? I feel they are numerous, but they are not generally externally obvious to other people. They are almost certainly obvious to those who understand the condition either subjectively or objectively in their own format. One of the essays I wrote for my Postgraduate Certificate was about the hazards someone with Asperger Syndrome faced in social situations. This is also so true for making friends because of the overlap involved.

Not only would I have to consider I how would naturally relate to other people, I would have to think about things like sensory issues, and issues relating to routines, structures and flexibility, amongst others. It is perfectly possible for me to relate to people, but the assorted background activities and a direct social approach make it much harder for me. A sympathetic group of people will be helpful in this as well as a great amount of concentration on my part. I have found it difficult, for example, to hear people during a conversation in a social situation and during various classes because of the background noise. This is not just a sensory situation, but information overload as well.

The cognitive deficits (Theory of Mind, central coherence and executive functioning) don't always help either, but this depends on the situation. Because I don't naturally tune into other people, I don't always see or acknowledge that they are in fact trying to help in a positive way (through Theory of Mind). This is something I find extremely irritating. Sometimes there is so much going on that it is difficult to focus in on a specific part of social interaction (central coherence). Furthermore, if things don't quite go to plan, what options do I have to choose from on the spot (executive functioning)? No wonder it is difficult to readily make friends!

Bibliography

Attwood, T. (1998) *Asperger's Syndrome: A Guide for Parents and Professionals.* London: Jessica Kingsley Publishers.

Rainman, film, directed by B. Levinson. USA: Metro Goldwyn Meyer, 1988.

Chapter 12: Social Relationships I've Had and From Which I've Learned

Vicky Bliss

Introduction by Luke Beardon

Vicky has a superb writing style and a great sense of humour. This chapter could easily be extended into a book, such is the richness of the writing. Vicky notes how she used alcohol as a coping mechanism (amongst other things) and while this may not be the best idea it is worth noting that everyone needs their own coping mechanisms, including time to actually be themselves. It is so often the case that people with AS have to spend so much time putting on a 'front' simply to get by, that there is little opportunity to genuinely be themselves. It is critical that individuals have the opportunities to engage in activities and behaviours that provide them with stability, however odd they may seem to the NT. Unless the behaviour is dangerous in some way acceptance is the key. After all, most behaviours are perfectly OK so long as the right boundaries surround them – and it is down to the NT population to ensure that such boundaries are in place and that the opportunities to engage in necessary behaviour are always available to the individual – be it at work, at home, or in the social arena.

I am writing from a personal perspective about the difficulties and successes I have experienced with social relationships throughout my forty-some years. It is only fairly recently that I have pieced together fragments of my early childhood memories in order to diagnose myself as on the autistic side of normal. What I want to do in this piece is outline the various situations in my life and then note the aspects of social relationships that helped me to cope and even more importantly to grow in my understanding of the social world.

My best guess is that I started out (pre-school years) pretty autistic in my thinking and behaviour. When I started school, aged five, I watched and copied enough behaviour of other children to squeak by as harmlessly odd, until I went into college at age 18. Without the comfort and routine of small town and family life, I soon depended upon alcohol (and lots of it) to (a) make me as stupid as other college kids, (b) dampen my anxiety in social situations and (c) give me a socially acceptable excuse for behaving oddly.

Through the grace of God or the fickle finger of fate, I managed to attain a Bachelor of Arts degree (oddly with honours in academia rather than alcohol) and I was off on my first real job. I took the first job offered to me that included a big, private office which happened to be as a social worker for people with learning disabilities. I had no idea as to what that job might be about, but the office was really *really* nice and they wanted to pay me for sitting in it so I was happy. Six years later I was on the move again with high hopes of going back to university to become a clinical psychologist. I tied my belongings into a hankie, tied the hankie onto a stick, and set off for the big city where I knew not a soul. Is this the behaviour of a right-thinking person? I suggest not, and it does get worse.

I was in a noisy, busy, expensive city with no income and no friends and, sadly, no entrance to university. I just managed six months, because my brother sent me money on a regular basis, and then I got a job as a social worker again. At least I had a role to fulfil and some rules to follow that probably saved my life, but I never paid my brother back the money he lent me and I never got on the clinical psychology university course. I spent several years as a social worker before being promoted to area director of a small community-based service for people with learning disabilities. I was in charge of a budget of $750,000 and about 45 staff supporting 30 adults with learning disabilities. Quite a funny turn of events for someone who can't balance her own cheque book, misses more social cues than she gets, doesn't like noise, lights or people and is pretty much a grumpy person.

After two or three years doing this, I finally got accepted onto a university course in counselling psychology so I moved again, found three part-time jobs to pay the rent, convinced the university to hire me so I could get my tuition free and set about studying psychology. My mother moved in with me and provided me with an anchor point so I didn't whizz right off the face of the earth with my frenzied activity. I was diagnosed as depressed, anxious, hypochondriac and then obsessive compulsive. I got engaged to be married and made all manner of wild plans. I was very thin and very manic which I suppose was handy so I could manage four part-time jobs and full-time education. I began a relationship with several different therapists. I was prescribed Prozac which resulted in me doubling or tripling my efforts to be normal so that I wouldn't be seen to be a 'head case' that needed medication. Instead of taking the drug I became even more manic. Funnily enough, my mother (who was living with me, remember) lost weight too. How the poor woman survived watching her daughter self-destruct is beyond me.

I finished my three-year master's degree programme in two and a half years (that's how fast I was moving!). I went on a two-week holiday to meet my uncle and his family in England and fell absolutely, irrevocably and perhaps unfortunately in love with the place. I didn't settle when I returned home, and within about eight months, I had secured a job in Manchester, England, sold most of what I owned and packed the rest into six boxes and moved across the Atlantic. I mean, would you? What a silly, silly thing to do, but at the time I couldn't see any difficulty with leaving all my family, my animals and my handful of friends so I could move 5000 miles away to a different culture where I knew very few people.

I was distraught, of course because I had not been able to imagine or plan for the considerable differences between the two countries. Luckily my auntie, uncle and lots of cousins lived close to where I had set up home and they were able to provide support and alcohol in sufficient quantities to get me over the very rough moments. I was also lucky to join a team of people at work who were extremely supportive and kind. I found it much easier to work as part of a team in England because my idiosyncrasies were attributed to my being American as opposed to being just odd. In a sense, I was expected to be odd and it was perfectly acceptable for me to ask a lot of questions about social behaviour and people's expectations of me. I think in retrospect, this was one of the things that made me feel so at home in the UK; I could be odd and fit in at the same time.

And it is here I have stayed. I came for two years only and it is now 17 years later. I remain hopelessly devoted to the country and to my fellow people who, for whatever reason, do not fit into the mainstream of society.

I do not fit into the mainstream of society and many aspects of 'normal' life simply elude me. I am old and cranky enough now not to care whether or not I am doing the 'done' thing or wearing the 'right' clothes or even whether or not I 'fit in' with the important people.

That is the backdrop against which I now talk about my experiences of social relationships. The majority of my relationships have been necessary as points of reference or anchor in my chaotic little life. Some relationships have been frivolous, some have been dangerous, and one or two have been with the devil herself.

Social relationships as a child

I had my way of being as a child. I made up lots of rules to help me understand and predict things around me. I was convinced I was right in my rules and people who didn't think and act like I did were simply wrong. I thought they would want to know this, so I frequently told people they were wrong and I was right, believing the resulting show of emotion from them only served to prove my point; they were illogical and not as smart as me. I guessed they were upset at their new discovery that they were wrong or stupid; it never occurred to me that they were upset because of something I'd said. It was my duty to tell them; I'd want to be told, wouldn't you? One thing that helped a little when I expressed a strong and hurtful opinion about something was that my mother seemed to explain the situation to me rather than to get angry or embarrassed by me. I would believe I had said something wrong because my mother was all-knowing and I trusted her without question. I would apologize if she said to, but later I would have to tell her that the whole thing didn't make sense. It helped that she used to say 'I know it doesn't make sense dear. Lots of things don't make sense'. She was my first experience of a really, really good listener, and that was very helpful.

During the early years at school, I think I was pretty easy going during unstructured time, so some of the kids seemed content to hang around with me at play time. We would play on swings, jump rope or twirl on the merry-go-round (I think the UK term is a 'roundabout'), but my favourite thing to play was cowboys and Indians. I was obsessed with *Bonanza* and even more specifically with Little Joe (the youngest of the Cartwright boys) and his 'paint' pony. During recess (play time) I was always Little Joe and others had to be Indians. I don't think there was a point to the game except to race around twirling pretend lassos and whooping. More kids stared than took part, but I didn't see anything wrong in this.

Social relationships for me, at this young stage, were about using people as objects really; means to an end. Other children fulfilled a need of mine so they were OK. If I needed an extra pair of hands to twirl a jump rope or to chase me as Little Joe or to explain an assignment, people were just fine with me. They were also useful as models I could watch and then imitate to see how what they were doing felt. I have no idea what they thought about me though. I don't yet know, even at this late stage in my life, what it's like for an NT kid to have friends at this young age. Maybe it's the same as it was for me, though I suspect it is a vastly different experience. I cannot actually think of anything my young friends or teachers did for me that was helpful during these years. It was my mum, dad and brothers that got me through early education.

One of my earliest memories about school was the feeling of genuinely 'not knowing' things. (This mindset, which I have nurtured, tended and grown all my life has become a cornerstone of the solution-focused work I do as an adult and I do believe it is one of the reasons people feel that I really, really listen to what they are saying in therapy – but that's a story for another time.) Because I have always had to really, really listen and watch and process and wonder and experiment and 'try out' different things in order to make sense of what other people were doing. I used to sweat (and still do) with the effort of listening and processing information.

As an example, picture this little scene: little Vicky, seven years old, clothes wrinkled and crooked as though hastily thrown on, standing facing the lovely, tidy, hair-combed Cherie whilst five or six other girls stood in a circle around them. Vicky's head is thrust forward, eyes narrowed and face grim as she stares intensely at Cherie, who is talking and gesturing away.

'You are so stupid,' she says with a laugh. 'You don't even know that your socks are supposed to match'. There is silence whilst Vicky's brain says 'Huh?' In an effort to gather more information, Vicky eventually says 'Match what?' where upon Cherie and the rest of the girls erupt with laughter. Vicky's face stays deadpan and despite frantic processing and reprocessing of information in her seven-year-old brain, she can make no sense of this exchange. Finally, just before running off to join a game with other girls, Cherie shouts back, 'Match what? Match your blouse of course!' and everyone runs off leaving Vicky standing; a stiff column of mental activity. I didn't feel sad or picked on. I felt 'not knowing'. Like an important piece of information was left out which, if found, would help me understand the 'rule' Cherie seemed to know but I didn't.

It was an exhausting few minutes, and after all the effort of processing information, I was no wiser about what I was supposed to take away from that exchange. I didn't let it drop though…oh no…my method of operation was to pursue something even if that meant climbing over the prone bodies of people I'd bored rigid with my obsessive information-gathering; adults and children alike, I would bore them, climb over their collapsed bodies and ask the next victim the same thing. I was ever on a quest to climb out of the 'not knowing' hole and to *know* something for a change!

It was Mum who got the brunt of this intensive questioning and I am prepared to believe that my behaviour caused a permanent change in the shape of her brain because she must have had to twist it around and around to keep up with the gist of my seemingly random, entirely private logic.

'Mum,' I started between mouthfuls of my tea that evening, 'what are socks supposed to match?' I didn't notice, but I remember being told, that she was in the middle of a discussion with my dad when I interjected this question. And she must have wondered, now and for years to come, what fold in my brain housed such random questions.

'Err…um…well, each other I suppose,' she ventured. 'I suppose socks are supposed to match each other.'

'What does "match" mean, then? Specifically speaking I mean.'

'It means that your socks come in pairs…ahh…and that they ought to be the same colour and same length as each other?'

I could tell she was sounding doubtful, but I didn't know if this was because she was fabricating an answer or for some other reason. I was suspicious. There must be more information which I don't yet possess I guessed. Cue more questions.

'How about your blouse. Are socks supposed to match your blouse?'

'Well, I've never seen that written as a law, but I guess socks could match your blouse, though nothing will go wrong if they don't match your blouse.' I think she knew better than to ask why I was asking these questions. I had observed that she often seemed to have a weak constitution for my pursuit of 'the truth' and there were many things that she must've figured she'd be better off not knowing. In any case I think that she was keen not to encourage more questions of this kind.

'Well,' I stated clearly, 'I think from now on my socks ought to match my blouses when I go to school. And of course they should match each other too.' And thus began a routine of worrying about things matching that came to be seen as a weirdness of mine when it belonged to Cherie all along! How unfair was that?! I now think Cherie was employing sarcasm when she said socks were supposed to match blouses, though there remains a nagging concern that I have missed an important social rule, and she might have been right. I find myself noticing socks and blouses even now, though I take no care with my own. I do notice such things on other people, just in case Cherie was right and everyone else knows that socks ought to match blouses. I doubt if Cherie ever gave that conversation another thought, whereas I made it a cornerstone of my development.

So, with the high number of 'throw-away' comments that people make every day, how is a person supposed to know which ones to pay attention to? I used to try to process them all, literally, which often left me overloaded, standing rigid whilst my mind squeaked away like a rickety hamster wheel. Mental files would be opened, discarded, sifted through or heaped in a pile until I could draw some kind of conclusion to the frenzy. I don't think people understood the magnitude of energy I was expending, or the reason why I would get so angry when people would make comments just for the sake of talking rather than to give information. I would spend all this time and energy processing what they were saying and by the time I could respond they had moved on, and I was the one who was thought of as weird or slow. Or, like the matching socks episode, they would make a stupid statement, which I would work hard to make sense of, and then I would be the one accused of obsessing on a detail! One can, I think, easily see how this interfered early on with the development of social relationships. What helped however, was again my family's constant supply of information for me in answer to my questions. Additionally, several of my brothers and my mum were particularly able to put things into a context for me which made information much much easier to process, remember and use.

Social relationships as an adult

The framework established as a child remained through adulthood. I was forever 'not knowing', forever taking whatever someone said seriously, forever processing information, trying to find meanings, associations, patterns or any structure that would guide me to some useful conclusion regarding what people said. I didn't know the importance of being able to run my thinking and my experiences through my mum's head though, until I moved out of the house and began a four-year Bachelor's Degree in Yankton, South Dakota.

I received a scholarship to attend the Yankton Conservatory of Music as a percussionist. Music was a 'thing' and I was quite talented with 'things'. In many respects this was a life-saving situation, being in music, because my first experiences of being away from home landed me with a small group of musicians who were, believe it or not, even weirder than me. I shared a room with a woman who was a positive joy to watch, she was so weird to my eyes. She was a cowboy, no doubt about it, and I had never seen one like her before. I unashamedly stared at her from every angle because she was so 'not me'. I kept saying 'She's not me' which of course was a masterful statement of the obvious. I think in the end I might have creeped her out a little. She went back home to the 'ranch' I imagined, after about four weeks of sharing a room with me. I was not surprised. She was just so 'not me' therefore she didn't belong where I was. It is a logic of a kind.

When I had a role to play, which I always did when playing in a band or orchestra, I amazed even myself with my greatness; possibly in retro-spect it would be more accurate to say I amazed *only* myself with my greatness though. I was among people who were musicians, not social creatures, and I loved it, though it did nothing to encourage appropriate social behaviour within the 'normal' world. That took alcohol.

I caught the attention of an arrogant, egocentric man who was studying business in the world outside the Conservatory of Music. He gave me flowers and made me laugh (only to make himself feel good it turned out) therefore I gathered that he liked me. He introduced me to one of his circle of friends who was studying to be a teacher, and lo and behold, she had the same brain as my mum! Not really of course, but she was a kindly, funny, thoughtful, insightful person who didn't seem to mind my constant stream of questions and observations. She coached me and taught me an awful lot about coping in the insane 'real world'. She never said 'You ought to know that' and at the same time gave me credit for being intelligent AND 'not knowing'. She seemed to know that a person could be both of those things at one time. And by 'eck could she drink beer! So, in a flash I abandoned music along with the weird people who had surrounded me and switched my major to elementary education so I could be with my new beer-drinking friends.

We laughed and threw up and luckily studied so we weren't all bad. What strikes me now about this is my need, at the time and even now, for me to pursue new interests with 100 per cent immersion. I abandoned music, which had been the love of my life, without a second glance and started taking real academic subjects like psychology, history, French (for God's sake! In the middle of the United States!) and maths. I had found someone whose brain I could borrow, who would look after me, who wouldn't let people make fun of me and I wanted to be with her all the time. I had a boyfriend too though he was more of a 'thing' than a person with whom I interacted. He was the 'thing' that bought the beer. I know. I am hopelessly romantic aren't I?

Latching onto someone else's brain was a pattern I repeated over and over through my adult life. In my mind, I have different periods of evolution; first was early childhood and school in Battle Creek Iowa. (Yes, that's really the name and yes, it certainly really was a 'circle the wagons' kind of cowboy town.) Next was college, then came my first real-world job and a cool, adult-looking office.

I was hired as a social worker for adults with developmental disabilities (called learning disabilities in the UK). They were absolutely great teachers and I felt quite at home working with them. What they did that was so helpful was to accept me just as I was. They didn't read anything into things I would say and they would be honest with their own opinions too. They were so easy to get on with. When Roger thought I was dangerous and crazy as a van driver, he said exactly that and asked to get out of the van. I loved that! I could converse with them without using anywhere near as much energy as it took to converse with their parents.

When Sylvia was hired about a month or so after me, I suctioned myself to her and she became my oracle for the next five years. What Sylvia did that helped was stay calm. The woman was always calm and she always looked competent. She always knew what to do and that made me feel safe and happy. She told me which guys fancied me (because I'd never even wondered about this), she taught me how to get guys to buy beer for me (it involved 'role playing' which again was a foreign experience, but with great pay-offs). She interpreted the bosses' moods, gave me contexts for information I was learning, and she pointed out the things I was doing that were just right (because I didn't always notice how my behaviour affected other people). She used concrete examples like: 'When you asked the manager how her decision to sack the van driver fitted within the company's motto of "putting people first", she thought you were pointing out a flaw in her character'. This completely threw me because I was only asking a question to further my own understanding. It was a genuine question, not a statement about anyone's character. Sylvia also stuck with me, and everything was fun with her.

I moved on to the big city after about five years where my brother and mother provided my sole means of financial and emotional support. And they were hundreds of miles away from me, so I was pretty desperate. I became an obsessive Catholic at this time, and also began seeing a man because he was handsome and wore a suit. I swear it's true. I was taking classes at the university too, so than routine was helpful. I did not have anyone's brain to borrow though and that left me vulnerable.

Fortunately I was hired as a social worker again, for people with learning disabilities and they set me back on some 'normal', safe course. People in the city had broader views than people in rural Midwest though, so I was treated to an entirely new set of rules and truths about life from some homeless, streetwise people on my caseload. They didn't mind teaching me, but they made it clear than their survival came first and I came second, which was really the first time I realized that other people have agendas that are not only different from mine, but are sometimes even more important than mine. In fact, the entire service was more wrapped up in agendas that didn't include me, so even my friend Ellen, who did her very best to support me, had only limited time to 'teach' me about living. It was life in the big city and after a few years of it, I moved back into a rural community. Frighteningly, I was the director of a small service for adults with learning disabilities. Luckily my mum came to stay with me quite often and she stepped in when I could find no other person to take me under their wing.

So how'd I get where I am today?

The established themes discussed above kept repeating themselves, though not because I orchestrated my life that way, that's just how things happened. I had a mixture of experiences and a growing base of information on which to build future experiences. Without consciously trying, I would attach myself to a likely, sympathetic suspect and lean heavily on them for feedback on my own behaviour, for explanations of others' behaviour, for contexts into which I could put newly learned information, and for reassurance that I was a worthwhile person.

Looking at my social development from an overall perspective, these are the things that have helped me to develop relationships:

As a child:

- attending a small school where everyone knows everyone else
- hearing messages from my family that I was unique, important and could do whatever I wanted to do (in terms of a career) with my life
- having a family home characterized by tolerance and humour
- hearing the message that things do not always make sense and that this is not because I am missing information, it just is the way it is
- having a family who naturally highlighted the things I did right whilst not getting too excited about the things I did wrong.

As an adult:

- finding people who repeatedly showed me that they wanted to be with me and that they accepted me
- repeated assurances that I was worthwhile and smart
- people who were patient when listening to my newest piece of information, and who had the ability to put it into context for me
- people who saw humour rather than horror in my mistakes
- people who pointed out how I was the same as other people rather than focusing on my differences
- people who kept an eye on me, even if it was a drunken eye, because perhaps they sensed the ease with which I could get into trouble through vulnerability
- people who let me make my own decisions, even if they didn't agree with them

- people who asked my opinion on things and made me feel important

- people who were quiet and calm and able to appear confident

- people who could put their opinions aside and really listen to my frame of references in order to understand why I was saying the things I was saying

- people who could accept my observations as valid, even when they were different from the norm.

To those people I owe a great debt. In a very large sense, I am not an individual, I am the sum of their kindnesses.

Chapter 13: Asperger Syndrome and Social Relationships: My Experiences and Observations

Anne Henderson

Introduction by Luke Beardon

I love the idea that Anne presents in terms of a template – and that everyone has to fit in with it. It seems so odd that NT society often describes itself as unwilling to 'label' people – and this is a reason not to diagnose. I see a diagnosis as exactly that – a diagnosis. I tend to find that without the diagnosis the chances are that the individual will end up with a whole long list of labels instead – naughty, selfish, rude, offensive – these are the true labels that are almost always inaccurate and highly detrimental. The world is not a place where everyone will be the same, ever – and the sooner this is recognized in terms of accepting the nature of AS, the better.

My son has Asperger Syndrome which was not diagnosed until he was in his late twenties and that was about ten years ago – long after he had left school. He knows that I am writing this and is happy for me to do so if it helps illustrate how difficult life can be for someone with Asperger's.

Social relationships are the most difficult to write about as they have caused such heartache and sometimes I just feel that they are the hardest part of AS for me or any NT to understand. I have been so lucky to have friends who have been wonderful to me, in particular my two oldest girl-friends, who have always been there for me.

For my son, too, it has been hard for him to understand the complexities of friendship, boundaries and all the nuances that just happen for people not on the spectrum.

I could give hundreds and hundreds of examples of our experiences, some fantastic but mostly difficult. As a very young child my son did not play easily with other children and was quite happy to be on his own – play school was really difficult for him – he was much happier in his own surroundings and school was even more of a challenge. As a family it was hard as we would be invited to visit but seldom asked again, except by people who accepted us as we were – it was about this time that I realized who really were friends or not and, to this day, I still feel sad that some people who were childhood, or close, friends of mine found it easier to walk away from us than stay friends. Even family have found Asperger Syndrome a difficult disability to be comfortable with. My parents were wonderfully supportive but it is sometimes hard for all the family; it comes down to not being able to understand unless you have actually had a similar experience.

As he grew older all sorts of problems arose – for example, he saw any woman my sort of age as a mother figure and could not understand when his familiar behaviour was misconstrued. He found boundaries and personal space a particularly difficult concept to understand and follow.

I could continue but find it difficult – I find that my carer friends are the people I can be really honest with about the frustrations and isolation of being a carer. I have to have other friends with whom I can be me but it has taken a long time to work it out.

My son is very sociable and, at last, after three years in hospital with the right help is doing well. He lives in a house with five others and is going to mainstream college and doing really well. All this has been achieved since he has been given appropriate support and both of us at last are happier than we could ever have imagined a few years ago.

My thoughts on social relationships are that in this incredibly material-istic society we live in we are all expected to fit a template and this is so difficult for someone with Asperger Syndrome. There are so many different ways of communicating and society needs to be made more aware of the complexities of Asperger Syndrome. However, at last more and more people are becoming aware of AS and I hope therefore that life will become more and more Asperger friendly.

Chapter 14: A Stranger in a Strange Land: A Journey Through the Social Weirdness of the Neurotypical

Cornish

Introduction by Luke Beardon
Cornish has a great way of putting things – if ever an NT wanted a good insight into how someone with AS sees the world then this would be a good place to start. I particularly subscribe to the perspective that if one were to view the NT population from the point of view of someone with AS then NT behaviour can come across as utterly bizarre and illogical. I do think that both the NT and AS population are both well equipped to commune harmoniously together; I also believe that for that to come to fruition it will take a lot more work from the NT population to learn and understand the nature of AS, and what adaptations need to take place before it can happen.

The big mystery – neurotypical socializing and interaction
For those of you who are going to be reading this, all I can say is, if you know nothing about the Aspergian genotype, and you know nothing

about the neurotypical genotype, you are going to be forever struggling to work out where you are going wrong. I'm an Aspergian, so obviously this nugget is going to come from an Aspergian perspective. So I'm going to give a few examples of what's out there…mainly in the form of observations and experiences, and a few Cornish conclusions…some of which I'm sure many Aspergians have already sorted for themselves…and how I've managed to get around the Aspergian socializing problem… So here we go, and we'll start with a few basics…

One of the main differences between the two genotypes is this: Neurotypicals live in a very complex social world, consisting mainly of ambiguities, with a metaphorical and vague mode of communication – basically it means they can cover their arses any time they need to. They need to live in a big social sphere of greyness, where they can change to the whim of the people around them. This means they can alter their own self-delusions to suit the needs of the many, and this gives them the means to adapt and fit in any time they need to. Fitting in is the main priority of any NT. Their allegiances will always be to whatever social preferences and cultural doctrines of the day, and are always peer led.

Aspergians live in the actual, physical world. This is a world that has no complex social filters. We may form opinions, but in the main our communication is based firmly around facts. We cannot process ambiguities, needing precise and accurate structure to minimize mistakes and confusion. Rather than socializing on a purely social level, Aspergians socialize on more of an intellectual level – reality as it is, in all its beauty and all of its ugliness – is very much the world in which we exist. Our allegiances will always (if uncorrupted) be to the truth, and not to the thoughts of others. If there is one thing I have learned: 'all facts are friendly': if you can't cope with facts, then it is you who has the problem. The problem does not lie with the facts, and that is a life truism. Our allegiances will always be to original thought, not to group mentality.

Here are a few examples of the differences between the two genotypes when they interact:

One day I was drawn into a discussion with a bunch of NT 'blerks' which took the shape of arguing with your nearest and dearest, and the old excuse of…'a good argument clears the air'. My immediate response to this is always 'What?' Why would anyone want to launch an attack on their most cherished, verbal or otherwise? Anyway the point is, I discuss, I do not argue. The thing is – I'm rubbish at arguing! Also, I find it far too upsetting. Like most Aspergians, I hate any sort of conflict. Therefore, I choose not to take part. I know there are plenty of Aspergians who do argue – that's not what I'm saying. However, my opinion was asked for, and something like this always puts me in a very difficult position, it puts me right under the spotlight…it leaves me with two answers I can opt for.

If I say…'Well I never argue with the one I love' (which, as I say I don't), then that is met with either, scepticism, or just plain hostility, because, unbeknownst to me, it seems that I've just shown whoever up to be unreasonable and not very caring – and that makes me out to be a bit of a tw*t…so I lose, even though the problem is clearly theirs.

Or, I can agree, which means I've just lied, which won't do, because lying causes me a great deal of emotional stress – it just has never sat well with me, also I won't lie just to keep a bunch of NT blerks happy – and so I lose.

In the end, I have to say nothing, simply because I don't want to take part in this self-justification game. But then this makes me out to be aloof and up myself, so you can't win whatever. I gave up trying to talk to mainstream NT males a long time ago…me an' Mr Blerk have never got on in any way, shape or form.

The other occasion was when I was out shopping. I had finished and was making my way to the check-out, when I came across two women talking in the aisle. They were stood near the check-out, but I couldn't see if they were in the queue or not. As it happened they weren't, but I couldn't see this. When confronted with situations I am not sure of, I usually wait and see what the outcome is. Suddenly one of the women turned to me and said:

'Sorry love, you should have asked me to shift out of your way.'

Well, I was horrified at this. On the way out, she was stood near the door waiting for her friend – I felt I had to say something, and had to make my feelings known to her, so I said to her: 'I'm sorry, but I think you have mistaken me for a normal bloke… I would never ever ask anyone to "*shift*" out of my way. I think you had better check out the sort of people you are hanging out with if that's the way you get treated.'

Someone later explained to me that her statement was a placatory one. I had taken it very literally, and had misunderstood completely. Still…this does seem to point out how the NTs expect to be treated…very sad really; and I wonder…is this innate? Or is this one of Piaget's schemata?… Who knows…?

Another time I was waiting to be served in my local paper shop. An elderly lady was stood next to me and insisted that I gave her five minutes of my time, while she went on about the obvious state of the weather. Come on lady… I've just driven down here… I've seen what the weather's like… Why do the NTs insist on stating the bleeding obvious at every available opportunity?

OK, so this is NT small talk that they use to initiate contact with and to pass the time of day – I understand this. However, when I wanted my five minutes reciprocated, and went on to tell about thermal weather patterns, their interaction with the oceans and the laws of thermal dynamics, she scuttled away as fast as she could, stating:

'Oh, I don't know anything about that.'

Well no, I wasn't expecting her to, but, 'eye for an eye' an' all that. My point is, the two information delivery systems are just not compatible…and when will the relevant people get to grips with this?

So there you go. On the one hand, you have everyday NT mundania, based more on partner incompatibilities…and therefore arguments ensue (so why not be honest and accept that you are with the wrong person), and on the other hand, it's the old rhetoric of how badly women have been and still are being treated by Mr Blerk, and once again, it's the allegiance to the social rules that formulate people's interaction with one another, and all of this is deemed more than acceptable, because no one wants to be seen to be upsetting the boat… Me an' the little old lady…it was pretty much a Microsoft PC and an AppleMac trying to program each other…*it just doesn't work!*

So, you must be able to fit in to whatever group which you want to socialize with. You must have the right mode of communication with all the right catch-phrases, slang and metaphors, dress in the way that all the other members do, and you must have the same opinions and prejudices, and be prepared to defend them at all costs. So get your hoodies, your heelies, your sweatshirts, T-shirts, Nikes, iPods with only the downloads that the group deems acceptable and forget about any form of individual identity. Basically, you will need to morph into the group mentality, and morph into the general group identity. Any decisions you make, must be the decisions that the group make as a whole… Do not attempt any form of original thought…to do so will get you immediately ostracized and ejected. Also, forget about the Aspergian mode of direct communication. You need to use lots of ambiguous contradictory statements, and hide anything you say under layers of implications and vagaries. The more you are able to do this, then the more popularity and social standing you will achieve...sorted...job done...mission accomplished...top banana...everybody bonded...baaa...baaa.

And so on to HONESTY...mmmm, honesty whilst conversing... The NTs have their own version of honesty...and believe me it's a lot different from the Aspergian one. The bar is set at an altogether different height than ours. What it actually is...is more like candour and not honesty at all. With NTs, you can only go so far, then there seems to be an innate warning system that kicks off, and that *is* as far as it goes...any further...and the 'bullshit' machine comes into operation, and does a very good cover-up job, and that's that.

What's happening is...the self-disclosure threshold is about to be breached, and no NT can afford that. According to a psychology tutor of mine, and this is someone who is an expert in the field...if everyone was totally honest with each other, then the world would descend into war and chaos (mmmm...take a look around...it don't look to be doing that good under the bullshit regime). According to Roy, the bullshit machine is what oils the cogs of NT social interaction, and keeps things running smoothly... which I sincerely question. The trouble is, when the bullshit machine kicks in, the NTs think they are still telling the truth. Now how f**ked up is that? No wonder there is so much distrust in the world when you can't rely on most of what people are telling you. If NT egos cause so much hostilities between themselves, I wonder why evolution thought it such a good idea. For example:

If an NT was acting like a complete 'dickhead', and someone informed them, then the informee would most likely get their lights punched out! If I was acting like a complete 'dickhead', I would want someone to inform me about it, then I could do something about it...what's so hard about that?

Personal disclosure. NTs are so used to making sure that no one gets any personal information on them, and put simply, they cannot trust each other not to use it to hurt each other. It's something they expect of one another. How many times has it been said that Aspergians are too trusting?

For a lot of us, we simply don't suspect that there's anything to suspect! This makes it very difficult for someone like an Aspergian, who doesn't naturally have an agenda to gain superiority over others, feel safe in a very dodgy world. And make no mistake, the main NT agenda, given the chance, is superiority over inferiority. NT history is littered with examples of this. It seems the NT ego cannot cope any other way. It seems pretty much immutable – and to me that is a major handicap. That way of thinking means there will never be a good and honest world for all – until the NTs learn how to behave themselves – it will remain that way.

The other main game that the NTs like to play is the popularity game, and ultimately who gives a f**k? This is a futile and worthless exercise. You are either a nice person who's worth knowing, or you are someone who just takes and takes and takes – a selfish bastard. Everybody else swims up and down in between, choosing what best suits them when they need it. This, it seems, is what you have to do to survive…can't see the logic in it. But if you need any pointers on this, then just watch a couple of series of *The Apprentice* or *Big Brother*, and this will show some of the best examples of how to be an NT.

So what did Cornish do to get around this utter nonsense, and get a social life together? Well, it did take a while, but I worked it out in the end. What it took was to ditch the social systems that weren't natural to me, and go where I was drawn. I have always been drawn to 'weirdness'…mainly the people of the 'subculture'. Not only that, I found that they were drawn to myself. Whenever I came across people that existed within little pockets of weirdness, I found I could always get on with them. Whether they were punks, hippies, New Age, freaks or geeks or whomever, I found I had some sort of commonality with them. Of course not every single one, but I tended to find in amongst them the sort of people who were my sort of people. They were the more tolerant, the more open minded, the arty folk, the musicians, people who didn't give a damn about convention and social conformity. People who didn't give a f**k about what anyone else thought…in a nutshell…sex and drugs and rock and roll!

Now I'm not for the moment advocating that every Aspergian should rush out and hit the 'rock and roll road to oblivion'…all I'm saying is, this is what worked for me. Although I no longer participate, like a lot of Aspergians (and NTs for that matter), self-medication opened up a lot of social doors. This was socializing after midnight, and off the mainstream radar. I entered this subcultural world at 20 years old, and have happily kept to it ever since. This was mixing with people who were very like minded. People who were disaffected like myself. People who were as pissed off with the world as I was, and just wanted to do their own thing in peace and quiet.

The irony of this (and yes, I do get irony) was that Thatcher's Britain enabled me to do this. I understood early on in life that my view of the world and my priorities were very different to the mainstream people in it. I didn't want anything to do with them, and they didn't want anything to do with me…and that suited me fine…everyone knew where they stood – cool. With high unemployment, this gave me the opportunity to step outside of the mainstream. So, the obvious and logical thing to do was to avoid contact… Although this led to a very insular existence…it worked for me. I had absolute control of the people in my life. Only the people I knew and trusted crossed into Cornish World. In fact, my house became known as 'Cornish home for the bewildered'!

But, OK, if you want to take part in the mainstream NT world, then none of this really applies to you, and if you are looking for an easy way to navigate and negotiate your way through the NT world of social gaming, forget it, there isn't one for Aspergians, so get real. It will always be a minefield.

A college tutor asked me once:

'What's the best things to teach young Aspergians so they will be able to get on in the world?'

After a pause for thought, I said:

'Well, if you teach them to lie and cheat, and generally misdirect people in everything that they say, treat others like shit, bully and constantly undermine and wind people up, and be a homicidal psychotic paranoid egomaniacs. Be petty minded, overly bothered in other people's affairs and try to get away with as much in life as you possibly can, oh and don't forget the overall "blag" to be the person you are not…then maybe…just maybe they might stand a chance…but let's bear in mind…this is the NT world we're talking about… NTs learn how to lie comprehensively by the time they are four years old…

…ooops, have I said something wrong?'

Well, obviously I had. But hey, I'm just telling it like it is, anything less and you'll be 'had' big time. Just remember, this planet we 'share' with the NTs is their world. We have to deal with their unfamiliar and unnatural ways. They have had thousands of years of sway over everything on the planet, including us and anything else that doesn't conform to their expectations. Also, remember, to a certain extent, they can't help being this way. Asking an NT to 'give their ego a rest' or to 'get over themselves' just isn't going to happen. Nature or nurture, it doesn't matter, they are what they are. Unfortunately for us Aspergians, and again according to my aforesaid tutor of psychology, the two main driving forces that motivate NTs, and in the main males, are…sex and aggression…held barely in check by flimsy frontal-lobe control mechanisms. This leads us to one of my main 'bees-in-my-bonnet'…and the term is 'challenging behaviour', that gets tacked on to any Aspergian that has an overload meltdown.

Now what happens in town and city centres on Friday and Saturday nights come the pubs and clubs kicking-out time…that's what you call challenging behaviour. Just ask any policeman or accident and emergency department. Just shows how flimsy the control mechanisms are…scary. This to a greater or lesser extent, is the 'wonderful' world of NT socializing, especially when you introduce alcohol into the mix!

OK, I know I've been somewhat generalizing, but these have genuinely been my experiences of mainstream society. NTs believe in some of the most illogical and damaging things that have constantly befuddled me over the years, and yet they hold tightly to them regardless of consequence: like weapons of mass destruction, the rise of Nazism and religion in any shape or form. But this is justified under the social adherence banner…just something to keep in mind. Also, these are the things that anyone who wants to take part in, needs to be fluent in. And yes, you really do need to know whose back to piss up, and whose back to stab…because at some time, you will be called on to do it. For myself…as I've said, I just didn't bother…I opted out.

As I write this, I'm at the 'thick end' of 40, and for myself, I stay strictly within the Aspergians 'envelope'. What I've found, is that, if I socialize with other Aspergians of pretty much my own functionality, then all of the so-called social impairments simply don't exist…we share the same operating systems, so there are no impairments…immutable logic.

Also, a very odd thing has become apparent over the years… People who I've totally 'clicked with', and who have become my closest friends, and I'm talking about people from 20-odd years ago (incidentally, I have only known about Asperger Syndrome since 2001 – diagnosed 2003), have in the past few years had children of their own, who now have either had an Aspergian diagnosis or are in the process of getting one, and *all* of my friends are now taking a closer look at themselves. Also, most of the people I have met since, or should I say, people who I have attracted into my sphere of existence if you want to get all New Age or whatever, have been Aspergian 'sleepers'. I no longer get surprised at this, as during my research, I have found that it has been well documented, that despite the fact that our numbers are small, we do have a tendency to find one another (cue the *Twilight Zone* music). Asperger Syndrome is my specialist subject and area of expertise, so it's generally the main topic of conversation with me. What I find is, after explaining what Asperger's is to these people, I am always met with exclamations of :

'So that's what's been going on with me all these years…'

Pretty much my reaction when I found out…

Groove on fellow Aspergians,

Cornish x.

List of Contributors

E. Veronica (Vicky) Bliss recognizes many, many indicators of AS in her own personal history, but the condition for her is as yet undiagnosed. She has worked for over 20 years with people who have autism as well as people with other differences and has worked as a solution-focused psychologist for the past six years.

Alexandra Brown prefers to be known as Alex. She lives with her partner and teenaged daughter in North Yorkshire. She has worked full-time for the past seven years within library services. She loves books but isn't always so fond of the people! Alex received her diagnosis of AS in 2007 at the age of 38. She enjoys writing, mainly for her friends, and uses writing to analyse her thoughts and make sense of the world around her.

Cornish was diagnosed with AS in 2003 at the age of 44. Since then he has become a qualified expert in AS. Cornish is an executive board member of his local autism charity, and has worked for the past five years with adolescents and adults with ASDs. He runs an informal telephone helpline and is part of an adult AS support group. Cornish is an experienced trainer, and speaks comprehensively on his own personal perspective of living with the challenges and joys of AS. Anyone wishing to contact Cornish can do so through the publishers (please do).

Giles Harvey was diagnosed with Asperger Syndrome in 1997 at the age of 22. He has had several jobs including working for a large charity in North West England that supports people with a diagnosis of AS. It was from this post that Giles developed a further interest in and knowledge of AS.

Anne Henderson's son had been labelled with every possible label and was eventually diagnosed with AS at age 27; he was sectioned under the Mental Health Act in 2004. After two years on a forensic ward receiving the right care he has moved into residential accommodation and has just started his second year at mainstream college. For the first time in his life he, his sister and mother are able to lead happier lives as he has appropriate support to achieve his independence and ambitions.

Liane Holliday-Willey is a psycholinguist who has authored several international bestsellers, including her autobiography *Pretending to be Normal: Living with Asperger Syndrome*, as well as *Asperger Syndrome in Adolescence: Living with the Ups, the Downs, and Things in Between* and *Asperger Syndrome in the Family: Redefining Normal*, all published by Jessica Kingsley Publishers. Liane has contributed to many additional books and journals, and serves as the webhost of www.aspie.com, a site dedicated to the understanding and support of Asperger Syndrome.

PJ Hughes is a civil servant. He was diagnosed with AS in 1999. He gives talks about his experiences and often writes articles as well. He is the author of *Reflections: Me and Planet Weirdo*, published by Chipmunka Publishing.

Steve Jarvis lives alone in Hertfordshire and has lived on his own all his adult life. He works as a learning consultant and has been in full-time employment all his life, but has never had any success with relationships. He was diagnosed with Asperger Syndrome (AS) when he was 45 years old.

Wendy Lawson, Bss Bsw (Hons), GDip (PsychStud), GDip (Psych), is an autistic adult. Being a partner, mum, grandmother and friend to so many occupies Wendy's time and gives her great joy and satisfaction. When it comes to the autism spectrum Wendy prefers the word 'diffability' to disorder and her research seeks to explore what being differently abled means in the world of neurodiversity. Currently, Wendy is working towards her PhD in psychology with Deakin University, Victoria, Australia.

Chris Mitchell was diagnosed with AS at university, at age 20. Since his diagnosis, Chris has completed his MA (Hons) in information and library management at the University of Northumbria, where he completed a dissertation on the impact of autism emailing lists. Currently, he works as a clerical assistant for an educational psychology service, and in his spare time is an advocate for AS, giving talks and workshops on the subject as well as providing training for potential employers and frontline services. His autobiography, *Glass Half-Empty, Glass Half-Full*, is published by Sage Publishing.

Kamlesh Pandya is a British Hindu Indian man born in Leicester, and was diagnosed with AS in 2005. He worked for the National Autistic Society, as a support worker in residential care with adults with autism, for over three years. He now works as an outreach support worker in the community and is a part-time visiting lecturer on autism and AS at De Montfort University. Kamlesh has had two girlfriends but neither worked out. He keeps to himself and has made some very good friends via the internet site Aspie Village.

Hazel D.L. Pottage, or Haze for short, has always had problems relating to others and in 1976 had a severe mental breakdown and was in an institution for three years. Already diagnosed with dyslexia and dyspraxia, she was officially diagnosed with AS in 2004. Her hope for the future is that, as AS becomes more recognized, life will be much easier for children growing up with the condition than it was for her, and that adults will be more accepting and tolerant of each other.

Neil Shepherd was diagnosed with AS when he was 31 after struggling for years to hold down a job in the IT industry, remain sane and do all of the things that 'normal' people do. Married, divorced and now happily living with his Aspergic girlfriend Emily, he is still struggling to hold down a job in the IT industry. He has also written a book about his experiences, *Wired Up Wrong*, published by lulu.com publishing.

Dean Worton has a positive expression of AS and lives in north west England. He has worked as a performance data administrator in the public sector for two years and has previously worked in a number of administration roles in the private and voluntary sectors. He is supported by an employment scheme for people with disabilities and in his spare time runs an internet social and support group for adults with AS who live in the UK.

Index

Asperger Syndrome and Employment

Adults Speak Out about Asperger Syndrome

Edited by Genevieve Edmonds and Luke Beardon

Adults Speak Out about Asperger Syndrome Series

Paperback, ISBN 978 1 84310 648 7, 176 pages

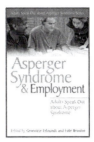

'This is the book we need for guidance on employment for people with Asperger's Syndrome. The contributors describe their employment experiences and offer sound advice. I thoroughly enjoyed reading the success stories and took note of the words of warning of what not to do.'

— Professor Tony Attwood

Employment is an important part of a healthy, balanced and fulfilling life but less than 20 per cent of people with Asperger Syndrome (AS) are in work at any one time. The adults with AS in this book explore the issues surrounding employment, providing advice and insights for others with AS, as well as their employers and colleagues.

Drawing on personal experience and lessons learned, *Asperger Syndrome and Employment* looks at:

- the transition from education to employment,
- the importance of matching skills to career choices,
- practical coping strategies for employees with AS in the workplace,
- advice for employers, including the need to make 'reasonable adjustments' to avoid discrimination,
- ways in which employment services ought to work for people with AS.

This is essential reading for adults with AS, their family and friends, employment services and career advisers, and companies needing to know how, in practical terms, to accommodate employees with AS.

A Self-Determined Future with Asperger Syndrome

Solution Focused Approaches

E. Veronica Bliss and Genevieve Edmonds

Foreword by Bill O'Connell, Director of Training, Focus on Solutions

Paperback, ISBN 978 1 84310 513 8, 160 pages

'Written with a light touch and plenty of humour, the authors use anecdotes and stories to show how people with AS cope in everyday situations and how effective understanding of a person's needs and goals is key to improving daily life for people with AS.'

– Human Givens

'A book which seeks to avoid treating AS as a problem, and aims to support people with the condition in succeeding in private life, education and employment.'

– BILD Newsletter

A Self-Determined Future with Asperger Syndrome presents an empowering, practical approach to helping people with Asperger Syndrome (AS) to succeed at college, at work, at home and in life.

The authors highlight how treating AS as a 'problem' is unproductive, and advocate a solution focused approach which recognizes and uses the strengths of people with AS to foster mutual respect and understanding.

Drawing on both their personal experience and knowledge of counselling, the authors use anecdotes and stories to show how people with AS cope in day-to-day situations. They also illustrate how effective communication and understanding of a person's needs and goals are key to improving daily life for people with AS. The final section of the book comprises practical worksheets and resources to help people with AS to recognize their achievements and work towards their goals.

This book is of interest to people who are affected by AS, their families, and the people who work with them.

E. Veronica Bliss has over 20 years' experience working with individuals on the autistic spectrum, and has been working as a solution focused psychologist for the past six years.

The Complete Guide to Asperger's Syndrome

Tony Attwood

Hardback, ISBN 1 84310 495 7, 400 pages

'An encyclopedia on Asperger's syndrome written in easy-to-read non-technical language…There is a good mix of research information, first person reports and clinical information. The section on sensory over-sensitivity is excellent.'

– Temple Grandin,
author of Thinking in Pictures and Animals in Translation

'*The Complete Guide to Asperger's Syndrome* is flawless in its ability to ease the trepidations, answer the questions, buoy the spirits, and encourage the dreams of those who walk with AS. Attwood and his insights are golden!'

– Liane Holliday Willey, EdD
author of Pretending to be Normal: Living With Asperger's Syndrome

'Tony Attwood explores in depth the complexity of the mysterious group of clinical pictures known collectively as Asperger's syndrome, part of the wider autistic spectrum. He describes all the puzzling and fascinating aspects of these conditions and brings them vividly to life with illustrations from personal histories. He has achieved real empathic understanding of children and adults whose basic problem is a biologically based lack of empathy with others. The book is to be highly recommended.'

– Lorna Wing

The Complete Guide to Asperger's Syndrome is the definitive handbook for anyone affected by Asperger's syndrome (AS). It brings together a wealth of information on all aspects of the syndrome for children through to adults.

Drawing on case studies and personal accounts from Attwood's extensive clinical experience, and from his correspondence with individuals with AS, this book is both authoritative and extremely accessible. There is also an invaluable frequently asked questions chapter and a section listing useful resources for anyone wishing to find further information on a particular aspect of AS, as well as literature and educational tools.

Essential reading for families and individuals affected by AS as well as teachers, professionals and employers coming in contact with people with AS, this book should be on the bookshelf of anyone who needs to know or is interested in this complex condition.

Tony Attwood is a practising clinical psychologist with more than 25 years' experience. He has worked with over 2000 individuals of all ages with Asperger's syndrome. He presents workshops and runs training courses for parents, professionals and individuals with AS all over the world and is a prolific author of articles and books on the subject.

Love, Sex and Long-Term Relationships

What People with Asperger Syndrome Really Really Want

Sarah Hendrickx

Foreword by Stephen Shore

Paperback, ISBN 978 1 84310 605 0, 144 pages

What are the motivations and desires behind relationship choices and sexual behaviour? Are they very different for those with Asperger Syndrome (AS) than for anyone else? Does having extreme sensitivity to physical touch or an above average need for solitude change one's expectation of relationships or sexual experience?

Many people on the autism spectrum have limited knowledge of how to establish or conduct sexual relationships: drawing on extensive research with people on the autism spectrum, the book openly explores such questions. For the first time people with AS discuss their desires, needs and preferences in their own words. AS attitudes to issues such as gender, sexual identity and infidelity are included, as well as positive advice for developing relationships and exploring options and choices for sexual pleasure.

This accessible book is an invaluable source of information and support for those with Asperger Syndrome and couples in which one or both partners has Asperger Syndrome, as well as counsellors and health and social care professionals.

Sarah Hendrickx is a Training Manager at Aspire, a project offering training for organisations and mentoring for adults with Asperger Syndrome in Brighton and Hove, UK. Sarah also works as a freelance trainer and consultant in autistic spectrum conditions. With her partner Keith, who has been diagnosed with AS, she is the co-author of *Asperger Syndrome – A Love Story*.